Views from
Lea Bailey

Views from Lea Bailey

ROBERT CHOULERTON

CP

THE CHOIR PRESS

First published in the United Kingdom in 2025 by
The Choir Press

ISBN Paperback 978-1-78963-559-1
ISBN Hardback 978-1-78963-560-7

For James and Elizabeth

Also by Robert Choulerton

Lines from Lea Bailey
Published 2022 by The Choir Press

ISBN Paperback 978-1-78963-271-2
ISBN Hardback 978-1-78963-272-9

Notes from Lea Bailey
Published 2024 by The Choir Press

ISBN Paperback 978-1-78963-424-2
ISBN Hardback 978-1-78963-425-9

Contents

PREMIUM   1
DECADE   3
FLEETING   5
PEDIGREE   8
REMEMBRANCE   10
FULL STOP   11
MIMICRY   13
TESTING   16
POPULISM   18
STARKITECT   20
HIGH-BROW   22
SMILES   25
PASSWORD   27
RIPPLES   29
MERIDIAN   32
CONFESSION   34
WEDDING BENEDICTIONS   36
KNOWLEDGE   37
COFFEE-MORNING   39
BETRAYAL   41
ACTING   43
CADAVERS   45
ERGONOMICS   47
PERSONA   49
MATRICIDE   51
ADRIFT   53
CHRISTY   55

PHILLIPS	57
HARRUMPH	59
PERSONIFY	63
CLOCK	64
WOODPIGEON	66
LORD'S PRAYER	69
NOUGHT	71
MASK	73
BERNARD KEAR	74
BRECON CANAL	77
EMBODIMENT	80
GRATUITY	82
TREE	84
PROTTY	86
SKY	88
MORALITY	90
CLOUD	93
MAKE-UP	95
TRAFFIC	97
FRAGMENTS	99
PARA BELLUM	103
INSEPARABLE	105
DIALOGUE	107
THE EYES	109
SCAPEGOAT	111
DULLARD	114
PETS	117
EURO 24	120
FACULTIES	124
PARISH CHURCH	126
FLY	129

SPORTSMANSHIP	130
LIBERTI	132
FEATHER	135
SALVATION	137
IMROPRIETY	139
DUVET	140
DADDY-LONG-LEGS	142
FJORD	144
HYPOTHESIS	145
SWEETBREADS	147
REVELATION	148
CRIMINAL	151
FLORA	153
"DOUG"	155
EXPECTATION	157
WATERFALL	158
CONGRATULATIONS	160
ENGLISH	162
WHEREWITHAL	164
BODY LANGUAGE	165
ALCHEMY	167
THE UNDERSIGNED	169
REFERENDA	170
CIGARETTES	172
MISCAST	174
CHRISTMAS	176
VILLAGE STORES	177
FISH KNIFE	179
'TOSCO'	181
SPINNING	182
RESTAURANT	184

TWO-SHOES   186
CONVERSATION   188
CARTOON   189
NOMINATIONS   191
ALIAS   193
CROSSING   196
EQUESTRIAN   198
FENG SHUI   199
FODDER   201
TEARS   204
ERNIE   206
ON AIR   207
SUPERLATIVE   209
SHAKESPEARE   211
ARMCHAIR   214
CATRINES   215
INSIGHT   217
MY BROTHER   219
CELANDINE   221
RED INK   222
PATRON SAINT   224
A I   226

Foreword

I offer my third collection of 'prosems', in the hope that you found my earlier books worth reading, and hoping that my personal observations may chime with yours. Life being such a jumble of the profound and the trivial, there is no general theme here, except in its being the honest reports from one person's mind – through which my own concerns and prejudices are plain to see. I guess such writing substitutes for friendly conversation: We meet on the page, where readers may compare experiences with mine.

PREMIUM

In those distant schooldays, well
Before (PT) physical training periods
Were elevated as (PE) physical education,
We were from time to time weighed
In the Gym, and had our height recorded.
Of little consequence was weight, but
A premium there certainly was, on
Height: I do recall, four feet seven simply
Felt subordinate, to four feet eight.
However spurious, at that time it just
Felt so real.
And now, in old age, I can affirm a similar
Petty satisfaction, in being 'more elderly
Than thou'. However vain, a distinct
Premium now, there is, on age. Each year,
It is a little more pleasing to respond to
A request for my date of birth.

Waiting, in a hotel lounge the other day,
I overheard an old fellow regaling his group
With reminiscences, twice or thrice impressing
Them with his date of birth –

"Twenty-second of November, Nineteen
Thirty-eight", he declared, as if to add heft
And wisdom to his words.
What was this quiet pride I felt, in knowing
That old fellow was, by one whole year,
My junior?
Some days later, once or twice, a phantom
Enactment formed in my mind, in which
Being one of his group – with all due
Respect and with consummate grace –
I trumped his subordinate Birthday Ace.

Oh, unworthy thoughts, get thee behind
Me – but not before I congratulate, flatter
And inflate myself, that I was even older
Than he, and forever shall I be.
Weight, height, wealth, fame, diminished
On the geriatric stage; all, in the end, must
Genuflect to age.

DECADE

With all the cultural and linguistic
Shifts I have witnessed in my time,
This word, 'decade', deserves to be
Listed. It had lain buried, but was
Resurrected some years ago, by
Someone airing it and wearing it –
A badge, I guess, of Latinate Learning.
Though its meaning is far from profound –
A period of ten years – some significance
Beyond itself, it seems to have accrued.

For see how 'over a decade', in all its
Vagueness, outweighs twelve or thirteen
Mere years; that we may appreciate
How numbers beyond ten, or groupings
Of ten, can carry impressive weight;
And that we may wonder how a
Reputation of 'sixty-five years' rather
Lacks this cachet of 'nearly seven decades'.

And maybe this word 'decade' has
Become, in the uttering, some stone,
A certain status and belonging, that
No educated citizen would care to
Leave untouched.

Inviting us to multiply by ten, in our
Minds, it has a tedious and unnecessary
Formality about it – no more tedious
And unnecessary, I suppose, than my
Writing about it – in which spirit I wish
The word 'Pentad', potentially 'Pentade',
A deep and permanent repose.

FLEETING

They pass, without our noticing,
A million times a day, these fleeting
Miracles, so commonplace be they.
Perhaps because we never see them
Slowing down; they are swift, and
Then they stop.

The garden hedge is an evergreen
Tangle of twigs and twists and snags
And spurs, kept in a kind of order
To represent a friendly border.
But to garden sparrows it is covert,
And base, and safety.
How busily they sally forth, to forage
Or bathe or socialise, several times
A day, but always sensing themselves
At risk, brief is their stay away; at the
Pace of a race, back to cover they dart,
Each miracle conjured before our very
Eyes, for never we see them slowing
Down; they are swift, and then they stop.

Suicidal, surely, is re-entry at pace
To that tangle and gloom, but in less
Than a trice they have folded their
Wings, angled themselves to pass a
Gap, opened out claws to clutch a
Landing spot and come to a perfect
Halt, with never a scratch or an eye
Put out, nor one feather out of place –
As if they've done it a million times
Before, which of course, in a way,
They have.

Or contemplate the common fly, when
It comes to land, on the back of your
Hand: You certainly will have seen, and
Probably never have noticed, that it
Does not need to skid to a halt, to steady
Itself, regain its poise. It is swift, and
Then it stops. From flight to stillness,
It defeats the human eye, those flimsy
Wings only to be seen, at rest.
Not only invisible in flight, even their
Slowing to stillness we do not see.

Such precision, I dare to say perfection,
In the common fly. Fleeting miracles
Indeed be they – passing without our
Noticing, several million times a day.

Now that the instruments of science
Can magnify, and slow things down
For the limits of the human eye –
Precious insights for the human race:
We are humbled by the natural world,
Miracles merely commonplace, helping,
Let's hope, to put us in our place.

PEDIGREE

Though I had not asked, it seemed I
Must be told: Evidently keen was she
That I should know – her level-headed
Daughter had chosen wisely, adding,
With a reassuring nod,
"He's a Shrewsbury Boy".
Scarcely aware of the existence of that
School, still less of its global reputation,
I gathered that she need say no more.
Those two words, 'Shrewsbury Boy',
Contain all that need be told, in
Themselves a guarantee of character
And worth; honourable, bright, manly.
For all I know, it may be so.

Along with pride and satisfaction in
The mother's telling, there seemed a
Sense of relief: At stake the family's
Reputation; perish the thought, with
A son-in-law from some lesser class
Of school.

The betrothal, one must hope,
Wholeheartedly the daughter's
Choice, independent of her mother's
Voice – but that their visions coincide,
A cause for such maternal pride.

What mattered to the mother, seemed
To matter to the daughter too; the
Daughter's fine discernment as fine
As a woman's could be: For lineage
And pedigree, none better than a
Shrewsbury Boy.
It may have been true, for all I knew.

REMEMBRANCE

Even as a loose and free assembly, to
March together, in the sheer force of
Numbers, is to unify, express and
Serve a common cause.

How much more unifying, with those
Marching feet at the drummer's beat,
Uniformly purposed, in step to the
Drummer's beat.

How much more, on Remembrance Day,
When the massed bands play those
Jaunty airs of yesterday, with a nation's
Loyalty and pride so choreographed
And unified.

Fervour, in the faces of those marchers,
Faith in this old country of theirs;
The Heartbeat of their Nation, no less,
This annual marching through Whitehall,
Mustered upon Remembrance Day,
At each November's Call.

FULL STOP

Delivered, as we find ourselves, in
Sentences of life, little wonder authorship,
Provenance or root, should linger in
A conscious mind, as open to dispute.

Punctuate however, by Fortune, Fame
Or Fate, no human sentence is unbound –
Upper Case to open, Lower Case to make
Some sense, uncompromising Stop to
Close, to go to ground.

Here, by this Stop, this burial plot, the
Disputation lies – this terminal event
Perceived through starkly differing eyes.

Inflexible, I fear, my metaphor, never to
Bend, to accommodate a person's personal
End. A blunt Full Stop, it would appear
To me to be, with nought beyond.

Hopes and expectations, beyond the
Grave, often will attend to a life well
Lived, rather as, in a reader's mind,
A sentence worthy of its writing, will
Overspill its ending. In a rational mind,
Moreover, plenty of room there is, for
Irrational hopes and fears.

For if authorship is perceived divine, in
Understandings remote from mine, our
Full Stop is merely a Comma, or perhaps
A Colon, anticipating blessings beyond.
I do not despise those differing eyes, for
With heavenly expectations, the dying
May well die in peace.

From my Earthbound way of seeing things,
I praise the work that Faith can do: While
Teaching of a life hereafter, its crucial work,
Its practical work, is here and now, in the
Living world, with the living me and you.

When we come to the end of our sentence,
Arrive at our own Full Stop, with comforting
Dreams of a Kingdom to Come, our destiny
Simply matters not: As far as we mortals
Ever will know, the wonderful work of
The Church will be done.

MIMICRY

What are these, this new-born thing
Can do – this prehistoric, feral cub
Can do – from the moment it is born?
It can utter cries for help; it can clutch
With a grasping hand. What faculties
Fundamental are these – to suck, to
Swallow, to see, to hear, to void with
Careless freedom, from its rear?
And whence those bodily organs,
Every baby furnished so, energising
Each and every baby so?
Developed over many million years,
The answers, it now appears, lie
Encoded, inheritance encoded, at
Molecular scale, egg within the female,
Sperm within the male.
Adaptation, many million years or,
As half this modern world insists,
Simply endowed by God.

Whichever it may be, for the likes
Of you and me, this new-born baby,
Ready-made, yet not quite
'Fait Accompli':
For here, for the like of you and me,
Here, for the sake of the human race,
Is the greatest task we ever shall face.

Ever, ever mindful must we be, that
Crucial to our destiny is this faculty,
So deep-inborn, of Mimicry.

Shall we present to the world, by and by,
A shifty, selfish layabout, an aggressive
Foul-mouthed lout, learning little and
Caring less, an anti-social fraudster,
Known to the police?
Or shall we present a good-hearted
Citizen, thoughtful and kind, well-read
And truthful, with a sense of fun, always
At hand to help people in need?

Some tendency, for all I know, may be
Pre-ordained in the genes, but let us
Be in no doubt – this man-cub has no
Option but to shape itself, model itself,
On the likes of you and me; such is
Our responsibility.

Until it is of an age to think for itself,
It cannot but emulate our conduct, our
Gestures, our manners, our language,
Our attitudes, values, habits, routines,
Our actions and reactions.
It is never long before we see, in our
Offspring, behaviour clearly derived
From the likes of you and me.

You knew all this, of course. Of that,
I have no doubt. But looking about me
In this world, it seemed worthwhile,
Once again, to point it out.

TESTING

To meddle with our microphones in
England's village halls, must be the
Very mission, purpose and delight, of
Every dedicated, mischief-making,
Audio-system Sprite.
Perhaps they do it out of boredom:
It must be a dull and dreary life, for
Technically minded local Sprites,
Loafing around village halls, waiting
For the next opportunity to enrich the
Village's Meeting Nights –
"Testing, testing, one two, three: Can
Everybody hear me?"

But where would village meetings be,
Without "Testing, testing, one, two, three"?
Without the imperfect, the intermittent,
The crackling; embarrassment all round,
And our Speaker, our Special Guest,
Smiling understandingly, politely unimpressed?

Where would village meetings be,
Without "Testing, testing, one, two, three"?
Without our sabotaging local Sprites?
For as monuments, of a sort, they stand,
Tributes in our native land, to such
Goodwill, with fallibility.

An uncontested fact, is it not, that
Never, in living English memory, has
An audio system in a village hall,
Worked properly, first time, if it has
Worked at all.

So praise the Lord, and Blessings Be,
To "Testing, testing, one two, three".

To all Committee Volunteers, everlasting
Praises Be.

And as to 'Testing, Testing' nights, may
All unworthy censure be confined, in
All forgiving frames of mind, to mischief-
Making audio system Sprites.

POPULISM

However 'ordinary people' may be
Defined, the term embraces, we may
Be sure, the greater part of humankind.
Since the Oxford Dictionary defines a
Populist as 'one who seeks to represent
Or appeal to the views of ordinary
People', we must admire that person
As, by definition, a democrat.

Websters has it as ' purporting to
Represent the rank and file of the people'.

Chambers puts it as 'one who believes in
The right and ability of the common
People to play a major part in governing
Themselves'.

Populists: Democrats all, by definition.
What could be more desirable, in a
Democracy, than a truly populist Leader?

But read any newspaper now, listen
To any broadcast, to hear any corrupting,
Self-serving autocrat dubbed as 'populist':
Exclusively pejorative now, in usage, this
Word – utterly misused, a blundering
Abuse of language.
They are Tyrants, crude dictators, not
Populists.

What accounts for this, I wonder?
Journalists, one hopes, must be literate,
Faithful to the language which is their
Stock-in-trade. Are they aware of this
Abuse? Do they not care?

We have made up words, in their hundreds
Of thousands, compiled dictionaries to
Set down all nuances of thought and
Feeling, to enlighten humankind, the clearer
To converse, worldwide.

Whoever would misuse words so
Wantonly, would edge us backwards,
Into darkness.

As to democracy, 'Populist' is inseparable
From 'Popular' with ordinary people –
Axiomatic as can be.

Who do these journalists, these politicians,
Think they are – that they arrogate to
Themselves the power to re-define words?
Or are they simply too ignorant to know
That they are doing so?

STARKITECT

It's not the architects who are troubling
Me, but the 'starkitects', the ones with
Spirit-level minds, apparently lacking
Souls; the ones designing breeding-boxes
Instead of homely dwelling houses.
The room I'm writing in, I'm told, was
Designed as 'Living-Room', but I'd scan
It in vain for any intimations of Life.
The starkitect's mind is an unfurnished
Room – rectilinear, his every thought.
Flat surfaces unrelieved, flat ceilings,
Straight lines, right-angles and rectangles –
Everywhere rectangles – fireplace, windows,
Cupboard space, floor space, walls, doorways,
The room itself; plan view and elevations,
Rectangles all.
Oh, how such unfurnished rooms
Expose and represent our very human
Nakedness, that would be dressed –
Calling to mind the very nakedness and
Plight of civilising mankind, primitively
Daubed on bare cave walls.

It falls to us then, in the starkitect boxes
Put out for us, to gather materials, fashion
And improvise, with fabrics and paddings
And linings, approximating to human nests –
Carpeting to soften the tread, upholstering
With rounded, more natural forms, to
Comfort the mind as well as the eye.

How telling, unsurprising it is, as I look
Around, to note the motifs, designs, brought
In from outside – on carpets, curtains, suites,
Wallpaper, tiling, blinds and ornamental
Vases: Why, it's foliage, and flora, endlessly
Curling and coiling – patterns of leaves,
Twisting stems, berries and blossoms of every
Kind, exotic, familiar or fanciful — forms
From a living world, progeny of growth and
Motion, forms from the comforting natural
World where even now, deep down, we
Surely still reside.

HIGH-BROW

It is in the context of music, that I now
Think back to that household, where
My late sister, my brother and I were
Raised. I think back to a father with no
Music in his soul, only regulations and
Duties. Our mother, as he, since infancy
Raised without ever much sustenance
For the soul.
If ever classical music was heard in our
Home, it was accidental, and brief: If
Ever our father – sole controller of the
Wireless set – switched on, only to
Release a snatch of orchestral music, he
Switched the thing off again, forthwith.
"They lap it up!" he would say, in a way
That fixed in our young minds a distant
Caste of benighted 'Weirdos' who would
Listen to such stuff.
Rarely even, was popular music tolerated.
Along with the hymns from school assemblies,
Memories of youthful music of those days
Come from outside our home.

We children three, were raised in a
Resolutely low-brow home.

Only in later years did I come upon
Classical music, learning not to be
Daunted by such terms as Symphony,
Concerto, Sonata.
As youthful music of its day served
Its youthful purpose, I was to find that
A maturity in music better served the
State of the grown-up mind: While
Much that I found, I disliked, much
Also was engaging, delightful, refining
And positively nourishing – Schubert,
For example, Tchaikovsky, Beethoven,
Puccini, Elgar, Chopin.

In later life, as a sensitive fellow ought
To do, I sampled opera, and came to
Know those Suffering Sopranos, those
Importunate Tenors, and their poignant
Arias, which every opera-lover knows.

Surprised was I, to find operas more
Appealing sung in Italian, than in English;
The magic lay in the music, English words
In that context, for me, a distraction.
These arias, I came to feel, sublime
Expressions of sentiment in the human
Voice, were what you sat though the
Rest of the opera for – much as a mundane
Life, highlighted but by celebrations.
Under the spell of music, they sing.

Similarly, as a sensitive fellow ought to
Do, I sampled ballet, where with many a
Graceful gesture, under the spell of music,
They dance.
Somehow, they sing and dance for you and
Me; somehow, it's music that sets us free.

For there sleeps a soul, within you and me;
There dwells some power in music, to
Waken it, to set us free.

SMILES

To awaken, in your new-born baby,
The promise of a baby kindling smile,
Is to kindle one more glimmer of light
In this, our human race – your motherly
Smiles, in a way, all as nourishing as
Your motherly milk – smiles, as it were,
To digest, at your suckling breast.

Self-evidently true, as it appears to me,
So many human faces seem never to
Have known this light, of that smile:
How this light is extinguished, who
Knows, but in countries run by cold,
Illiberal dictatorships, smiles become
An endangered species.

A recent press photo of the Chinese
President's visit to the US showed both
Presidents side by side.
President Obama, in tuxedo and bow-tie,
Is beaming broadly, his left hand raised
In salute to the onlookers.

Xi Jinping is standing stiffly, his
Buttoned-up tunic matching a face
Unable to smile, his features seized
In a constipated cramp.

Much the same, in the public faces
Of totalitarian leaders all, in all their
Humourless regimes. Yet cultural
And endemic, as such clouded faces
Seem to be, how hard to imagine
Young mothers, throughout their
Lands, staring at their new-borns
With such indifferent, stony faces,
As if to inhibit any tendency to smile.
Pernicious indeed, would a culture
Have to be, to sour the love between
A mother and her new-born child.
Not that we, in the less-inhibited West,
Are totally immune. Hardly a week
Goes by without 'mugshots' in our
Press, of men convicted of brutal crimes,
The word 'mugshots' about right to
Depict faces utterly starved of smiles.

Very little, on the face of it, lies between
Criminality, and inability to smile.

Oh for the Lighter of humanity, to prevail
Against the Darker.

Criminality or Culture, both somehow,
In their human way, able to obscure
Those kindling lights that must shine
Between each new-born baby and
Its mother's loving smiles.

PASSWORD

As people, so often these days, are
Encouraged to do, I went 'On-Line' –
For this was the simplest, the slickest
Way for a fellow to order some plants
For his garden.
The 'On-Line' site demanded to know
My title, name, postal address, but also
My e-mail address and compulsorily,
Mysteriously, my 'Password'. Password,
With a provision to help in the event of
'Forgot Password?' That it did not demand
My date and place of birth, nor my
Mother's maiden name, I was much
Relieved to find.
Quite a few people, I imagine, are apt to
Forget their Garden Plant 'On-Line'
Purchase Password.
Forgotten it, I had not; ever dreamed I
Should need one, I had not: To get into
MI5, GCHQ, Fort Knox, NATO Headquarters
Understandably, but to buy some
Lilies and begonias?

I did not even need a Password when
I appealed to the Lord Above:

"Dear Lord", I pleaded, "Forever will
I believe in you, and worship you, if
You can set me free, set this whole
Forsaken wide world free – from
Stifling officialdom, from Puffed-Up,
Petty, Punk Pomposity".

The Lord Above hesitated, and seemed
To shrug His shoulders:
"Bob", He lamented, "I know the feeling;
It's a bit like that up Here. Even if you
Believed in Me, I'm not sure I could be
Much help. Omnipotence is limited,
You know. Most things I can command,
But the purchasing of garden flowers?
Without a secret Personal Password?
Far, far, beyond My powers".

RIPPLES

To hear is not always to listen; often
Our thoughts are elsewhere, with the
Radio on in the background. Whether
Or not we listen, the radio retrieves
For us, acoustic ripples in the air,
Within our capacity to hear.
Way beyond our hearing, pervading,
Permeating universal space, are ripples
Of a different kind – electromagnetic,
Spreading mysteriously, at the speed
Of light – some indeed, constituting
Light, to take advantage of which, over
Deep Time, our two eyes have evolved.
Some primitive creatures, in dark
Underground caverns, have developed
No eyes; no need, for there are no
Ripples of light. To emulate those beyond
Our sight, we use transmitters of such
Ripples, harnessed with our words and
Music, and radios to convert them into
Acoustic form – to take advantage of which,
Over Deep Time, our two ears have evolved.

Whether or not the radio 'listens' – is
Switched on – the words and music,
In untranslated form, fill not only this
Room, but propagate far and wide.

Evidently, there be resonances of a further
Kind, through what medium I fathom
Not: Ripples of Religion, the various
Gods not the source thereof, but the
Visions thereof, as far as I can see.

Maybe, in people of Faith, that very
Faith is predisposition similarly endowed,
Over Deep Time evolved, as with ears
And eyes – following, as it were, some
Scent of Truth, or more literally Ripples
In the Earthly air around.
Let us say half of mankind has some
Faculty of sensing that to which the
Other half is deaf; some way of perceiving
Lights Divine, to which the rest of us
Are blind – Ripples of Hope adorned as
Faith, as it may seem to us.

But who can deny the adaptive faculty,
This embryonic faculty, that has grown
Within, and characterises mankind? The
Compulsion of Religion can hardly be
Denied.

So intrinsic seems Religion to the human
Soul, it must, necessarily, have the capacity,
Over Time – Deep, evolutionary Time – to
Sub-divide our species, over Ripples, into
Two, as similar, yet divergent as are frogs
And toads.
How confidently, peering ahead I see,
Amphibious folk resembling you and me –
Frogfolk, with hops and leaps of Faith, to the
Ripples a-godding: Toadfolk, to the Ripples
Oblivious, a-crawling, philosophically plodding.

MERIDIAN

It may be, for all I know, but verily
I doubt it so, that people living in the
Middle East locate their region in
Those terms. I doubt that the Japanese
And Chinese ever employ the term
Far East for their ancient homelands.

'Far East', 'Middle East', imply some
Point, well to their West, some Datum
Centre from which they would seem to
Derive – the terms 'Far' and 'Middle'
Quite natural to early adventurers
From Europe.

As a pupil, learning some History, I
Imbibed a sense of national pride.
Geography too, seemed to be on our
Side – as, no doubt, with pupils in
Classrooms far and wide.
Loosely, of the 'West' we refer to
Ourselves, but West of what, or where?

We had been spreading ourselves
Across the globe well before Eighteen
Eighty-four, but since that year we
Are West of nowhere; we are at the
Very centre, the core:
From pole to pole we imagined lines
Of Longitude, down around our globe,
All points on the globe being located
Up to 180 degrees West or 180 degrees
East of the Nought degrees Meridian
Line, right through here, at Greenwich:
The Centre of all, was Ours.

How tempting then, to extrapolate,
With time-zones all around the globe
Relative to, referenced to, Ours. The
World does, from our very British
Shores, so gratefully radiate.

With tongue-in-cheek, I speculate, as
A dyed-in-the-wool, patriotic devotee –

But might it not be, that just this chance
Wedding of Science and Geography, this
Pole to pole Meridian through Greenwich,
Hath begotten national self-importance —
A sense of world responsibility, commitment
To world affairs, and this very British Psyche,
Ineradicable, I'd say, in you and me.

CONFESSION

Inside a cake-tin, on a bed of cotton-
Wool, lie four birds' eggs I came upon
In recent years: The pheasant's egg,
Apparently abandoned, I found beside
A country lane; the great tit's left in my
Nest box after the others had developed
And flown; the dunnock's from an empty
Nest in my garden shrub; the thrush's
Left intact upon my flower border, I
Know not how.

Though they are so commonplace, so
Disposable in this reproductive world,
I have to keep them: They are perfections,
Commonplace perfections, exquisitely
Formed, flecked and tinted – to this
Natural world innate, such that all our
Finest painters study, in vain, to emulate.
Who could crush them and dump them?
Not I.

Miracles are they, not in the supernatural
Sense, but in that sense of awe, and wonder,
When in quiet moments we contemplate
This natural world.

Opening that cake-tin, I must confess, also
Releases memories – of my boyhood, in
Rural Wiltshire.
Those were pre-television days.
Those were pubescent days; those were
Short-to-long-trousers-starting-senior-
School-days. On weekends and school
Holidays, what did we do?

"Washwedo Safto? Tree climbin'? Explorin'?
Goal scorin'? Scrumpin'? Bird nestin'?"
In springtime it was likely to be bird-nesting.
Shame on me; I collected birds' eggs, as no
Doubt did many youngsters up and down the
Land. I had around twelve to fifteen, as I recall,
Some of them 'doubles'.

I learned much about wild birds, their
Nests and their eggs, having little sense
Of the damage I was doing. One Big Kid,
Who knew all about birds, said it was OK
To take one or two eggs, because hen-birds
Can only count up to three.

A cake-tin of memories: I could wish for
A bed of cotton-wool for my guilty conscience.

It is my boyhood contribution to that of which
We are reminded, almost every day – our
Depletion of the natural world – very likely
Why I simply cannot throw these four eggs away.

WEDDING BENEDICTIONS

Elizabeth, 2007
That all your hopes will ripen on the vine,
May the sunlight of good fortune shine,
And such a harvest may you press
From grapes of loving kindliness –
A marriage rendered thus benign,
Its cellar full of vintage wine.

James, 2008
Such loving friendship holds at bay
Misfortune's most tempestuous day –
For care and kindness, walls will yield,
With stones by trusted mortar sealed,
And rugged timbers, truth will hew,
As warmth and humour furnish through –
So spreads companionship its roof,
A marriage-house forever proof:
Then come what hail, come what rain,
Those winter storms will beat in vain.

Dad

KNOWLEDGE

To contemplate all that is not known,
Or never can be, is to stifle expectations;
That much is plain to me. Besides the
Unknowable vastness, how laughably
Little can be known.

Intellect being, principally, that which
Distinguishes our species, in our dread
Of not knowing, such irony inheres; the
More we know, the less we seem to understand.

As a human without knowledge, intellect,
I am a trunkless elephant, a bat with hearing aids,
A stammering auctioneer. See how perennially
Popular are quizzes, general knowledge tests:
In recalling facts there is such kudos, such
Status in mankind.

In my room therefore, witness to my insecurity,
There are bookshelves – Atlases, Anthologies,
Dictionaries, Histories, Synopses, Bibles, Digests,

And furthermore, a parade of
Encyclopedias stands guard, as it
Were, against philistine forces of
Ignorance. No matter that several,
I'm sure, from the rank of Britannica,
Have never even been opened; they
Have stood faithfully to attention there.
This boundless knowledge is mine,
Available on demand – kudos and
Authority, vicariously mine.

Yet I sense the limitations, however
Compelling facts may be, and comforting
To be so well informed – for here is
Vanity too.

I remind myself that facts can be as
Shallow as fame, however admirable
The quest: Behind human kindness,
Courtesy and grace, factual knowledge
Always trails a distant second best.

COFFEE-MORNING

With apologies to the coffee, which is as
Good as any you may find, I doubt it is
The coffee, as I doubt it is the cakes that
Volunteers generously bake – which on
The first Wednesday of every month
Draws people here, to the Lea Village Hall.

Incidental, are coffee and cakes; they surely
Are the welcoming pretext for something
More – for community gathering, company
And belonging.

Twenty-nine people, this morning there were:
Thirty later, when the rector popped in.
'A good turnout', they said, and from such a
Small village, so it was – typically, female
Outnumbering male by more than two to one –
Most, well into middle-age or elderly.

Two or three, content to be in company, would
Rather listen than talk, while the Hall makes
Way for and resounds to the animated buzz
And chatter of the village; it is The Village Hall,
After all, for company, and belonging.

A friendly informality is the order of the
Morning, with villagers catching up on the
Latest, from the more tentative talkers, to the
Robustness of Chris, whose bouts of bogus abuse
Merely highlight her cheery warm-heartedness.

An endearing social ritual is here: Twenty-nine
People, each with a tale to tell and so many
Lessons learned from their personal journeys,
Drawn together, leaning forward, the better to
Tell and be told, experiences shared and compared.

And what else, to round off the morning, but that
Very English and community way, of raising funds,
The Raffle. Jean won a candle in a jar; I won a
Packet of Ryvita.

So many such community events, these
Days, have to scale down, or be abandoned,
For want of volunteers – as very likely
Would these coffee-mornings, were it not
For the likes of Gill and Nigel.

What gratitude we owe to such as they:
The Dynamic Davis Duo – Gill will fulfil,
While Nige will oblige; Gill the provider,
With Nigel beside her.

BETRAYAL

We must be the only creatures on this
Earth to stuff our babies' minds, from
Birth, full of monumental lies; Far from
Alerting them to dangers hidden in the
Dark, lurking in the undergrowth or
Hovering in the skies; far from sharpening
Their reflexes, lessons in survival, training
In evasions and disguise, we prefer to
Stuff their innocent infant minds with
Monumental lies.

Nothing to fear, we beam at them – the
World is a cosy bed and fluffy nursery
Full of teddy-bears and tinkling bells.
You are the very centre and purpose of
This jolly, cuddling world, with endlessly
Patient and loving Mummies and Daddies
To feed you and clean you and keep you
Amused, and when you're a little bit older
We'll read to you, all about Wonderland
And Fairyland.
It may be healthier, you know, to tell
Our babies the plain truth, right from
The start – make it clear, right from the
Start, that every baby is surely going
To die: Even before they can read, show
Pictures of coffins and dead bodies; rock
Them to sleep not with lullabies, but with
A requiem about funerals and burials and

Resting forever in Peace.
Cut this baloney about life being joyful;
Death being sad; if you weren't supposed
To die, what was the point of being born?
Wasn't dying the whole purpose of living?

It may be better you know, to get to the
Truth, start with the Truth – blow away
All this frothy Wonderland and ever-sunny
Pantoland of silver bells and magic spells,
Humpty-Dumpty, frog princes, golden eggs
And Puss-in-Boots, godmother fairies, jolly
Farmer Giles, Mary, Mary, quite contrary,
Cows that jump over the bloody moon, and
Merry milkmaids all in a swoon.
(Look, I have to confess, that deepy, deepy
Down — I mean really, daffydown dilly, deepy
Deepy down – I've longed for all this to be
True, but I wouldn't let anyone know, excepting
You.)
It may be better, healthier you know, to tell
Our babies the sordid Truth: Godmothers have
Bad teeth and smelly breath, jolly farmers
Die of syphilis, and milkmaids get haemorrhoids.

Instead of pretending, when they grow up to
Smile like idiots all the time, let them face the
Grim facts with stoical, granite faces, and chant
Funereal dirges, in humourless monotone
Plainsong; show some courage, defiance and
Maturity – Death is Death; Nature buggers
Everything up; and God does sod-all about it.

ACTING

Elsewhere in the world, it may have
Differed, but our culture, hereabouts,
Inherited for women a distinctly lesser
Status than their menfolk; even in law –
Law largely decreed by men – women,
However much respected, were subordinated.

In property-owning, employment, voting
Rights, women restricted or denied. Divine
Endorsement, no less, was enshrined: Even
Now, in the Anglican Book of Common Prayer,
A 'promise to obey' is available, though
Rarely evoked, in the marriage vows of a
Bride. Feminism's rising tide then, to be
Welcomed, and hardly a great surprise.

As so often, in the pushing open of doors to
Rights and freedoms, there is creaking from
The hinges, a silliness or lunacy hanging
Around the fringes.

Let me take a representative lady,
Personifying this fringe. You will
Recognise her straight away, from
The stage or on the screen, for she is
Of the acting profession. Sanctified
And proud, she stands upon the very
Summit of noble, feminist principle.
I must confess, in referring to her as a

Lady, and using female pronouns, I am
Slavishly caving in to fusty convention.
For she is an Actor. Yes, an Actor.
For what could be more demeaning, more
Belittling or pejorative, than referring to
A female who acts, as an Actress?
I baulk even at using that word 'female'
For fear of treading on her neutral, or manly toes.

I can reveal that it was delivered by caesarean,
Of a loving father which was itself an Actor, in
The reign of our late King Elizabeth and its
Consort the Duchess of Edinburgh, that at its
Nuptials it was the blushing groom, obeying
Nobody, and that its children, of both genders,
Are neutral. And here it proudly stands, apparent
Strength exposed as weakness, forfeiting and
Leaking sympathy for the hard-won feminist cause.

I can further confirm that an Actress, stubbornly
Referring to herself as an Actor, is too deluded
And unaware, to see that she is being pompously,
Conceitedly, blindingly, superciliously, mind-
Numbingly, Silly.

CADAVERS

On just four occasions, with a few years
Between, have I been in the presence of
A corpse — cadaver, as it is gauntly known.

I went with my father, to view my mother's
Corpse. Not in a coffin, she was on a kind
Of plinth, in the funeral parlour.
She looked more composed and serene than
I had ever known her, brushed up, made up;
Lying in state, as it were.
"Well there y'are Vi," he said, "All yer worries
Are over now mate."
"I'm g'ner kiss 'er," he said, hoisting himself
Up and, with a tenderness I had thought
Beyond him, briefly did just that.

On the following three occasions, I was on
My own, to view my father himself, my sister,
And my late wife – all 'shrouded', rather than
Displayed, in their coffins.

Reduced to this, my father, a complex,
Nervous, inadequate man, mostly unaware
Of himself; in public isolated and all but
Mute; at home a brooding swagger about
Him, clearly in charge of a submissive wife
And three subdued and cautious children.
Harmless now, and free – rather drawn
And shrunken, in his repose.

Reduced to this, my sister, silent, sad and
Undervalued by a father who showed no
Love to her; a promising seed that fell on
Stony ground. Inhibited from childhood,
She then fell into a deeply disappointing
Marriage. Escaped and liberated now, eye
Sockets sunken and purple, head tilted
Unnaturally by that gross tumescence at
Her nape.

Reduced to this, my late wife, unaffected
And affable by nature, resilient despite
Early widowhood, untimely demise of
A brother, and her own ill-health.
In her repose now, womanly still, her
Starboard eyelid remains slightly ajar.

Such visiting, in itself curious enough,
It may be thought – an explanation I
Cannot supply – but people do strange
Things, don't they.

At each coffin, I felt the need, lightly,
To touch the one hand that was left
Uncovered.

There is nothing so cold.

And people think strange thoughts, don't they,
Such as whether anybody might, lightly,
Touch my one uncovered hand.

ERGONOMICS

How pleasing it is, when you're out and
About, to find places 'customer-friendly'.
Always they should be, of course, but so
Often are they not, that a customer-friendly
Place does stand out.
Warmly greeted we were, at the door, shown
To our table, provided with menus. The table
Was spacious, clean and firm, complete with
Condiments and napkins. The lighting was
Gentle, the background music soft and pleasing,
All staff efficient and courteous. The food and
Wine were excellent. All was well, except for
A deficit here and there – in ergonomics.
Often, single chairs are to be found, that are
Friendly and welcoming to a sitter – with a
Twin, shallow, ergonomic scooping of the seat
Anticipating buttocks and thighs.
A long bench seat at a table for two does not
Lend itself to this, but some cushioning would
Be a pleasant surprise, accommodating to the
Buttocks, and to the thighs.

The chief ergonomic deficit there, however, is
Commonplace, almost everywhere: Clumsy
Cutlery, irrespective of what you may order.
This mass-produced cutlery must have had a
Designer, but a designer without much thought
For any future, human diner. It matters not so
Much in the spoon or the fork, but oh, how it
Matters, in the handle of the dining knife.

The feel of cold metal is bad enough, but it has
Been factory-stamped-out, to function for a
Mechanical 'thing', certainly not for a 'whom':
Thoroughly mass-produced to slot into some
Insensate, robotic goodness-knows-what, it is
An insult to the human hand. Simple, friendly
Ergonomics, I plead; a handle of bone, or horn,
Or synthetically moulded, shaped and formed
For the palm of the human hand.

Such reform would spread joy, and satisfaction,
Around our blessed, customer-friendly land.

PERSONA

When the curtain fell, at the end of
My working life, it marked just fifty
Years of paid employment, and so I
Should have been surprised at how
Easily that mask, that persona, slipped
Away. All those years upon that stage,
As it were, adapting to various parts;
Fifty years other than myself, in Dramatis
Personae.

For so little, in childhood, had prepared
Me for that stage – no metamorphosis
Through grub and pupa to a crowning
Magnificence – some 'persona' it had to
Be, at the dimming of a promising childhood
Light.

Instead, for a working lifetime, the lights
Of artificial stages, the masks, the costumes,
The lines to learn, beneath which an essence
Of myself lingered, and shadowed.

Recollections and glimpses of myself
Along the way there were; though brief
And shallow, always, always young.

And now, with what ease do I uncover
Myself again, so much older now, but
Young still, at heart, answerable to none
But my conscience. Sad, some, I muse –
Our working lives, such a masquerade.

Myself again, something of that young
Boy again, at his garden pond. What for,
This pond, but to gaze and ponder, watching
The frogspawn coming to life; what for,
Our deeper, figurative pond, but to gaze
And ponder, reflecting on the past, the
Present, and whatever lies yonder.

MATRICIDE

It seems forever, that this old planetary
Cow has, as it were, been suckling – this
Providential matriarch, grazing in the
Pastures of our sun, forever has been
Yielding such abundant life.

All the more alarming then, to sense now,
Within our mother Earth, disturbances, and
Distress. Well may she swish her tail, flap
Her ears and twitch her flanks, for she has
Become unwitting hostess to pestilence
Intolerable, a kind of living plague.

Of her very own progeny, it appears, certain
Have turned upon their milch-mother cow,
Burrowing into her hide, gorging of her energy,
Supping vital juices – poisoning the mother's
Veins, polluting the very air she breathes.

Of her own progeny – insatiable species, upon
Its very own parent, parasitic.

How such a species, articulate and
Conscious, could evolve, to turn upon
Its own provider, is a conundrum, in
Irony, only that species itself can solve,
For faintly, through its madness, a
Certain common sense, now and then,
May be heard.

Not only do they proliferate, and swarm
Without restraint, in doing so, many other
Kinds do they trample on, and suffocate.

More irony, more astonishing still, and
Against all nature it seems, this insatiable
Species, further to its matricide, routinely
Destroys its very own kind.

What earthly organism would seek to destroy
Its suckling mother, the other forms of life
Around it and, meanwhile, itself?

ADRIFT

So long as we persist in dressing up
Humanity as the Blessing of the Earth,
The very pinnacle of natural goodness
And refinement, so long will we postpone
The search for some way to a fulfilment
And a peace.

Should we regard it as a gift, whatever
It was that cast us so adrift? Less a gift,
I suspect, than randomness and circumstance.

Out upon oceans of language and imagery
Do we drift, bereft of bearings, able to grasp
One thing only by relating to another.
A fickle faculty is language, for only metaphors
Will do, and they, for all their abundance,
Too few, it seems, to grasp what otherwise
Lies beyond our reach. Adrift, in a context
Of our own, we had better band together in
Groups, as for safety and some purpose, pay
Obeisance to constancies like the moon and the sun.

Never having been out here before,
Knowing not which way to turn, nor
Any sense of destination, we follow
Mystics, gurus, spells and incantations;
Philosophies and scriptures, banners
And flags of charismatic leaders.

For all these charismatic leaders, who
Have never been here before, and know
No more the way, the destination, than
Do we, we might as well be thankful:
So long as we find, through them, comfort
And reassurance, what matter, so limited
Seem the options.

CHRISTY

To write of a good friend, is quite naturally
To emphasise the virtues, and respectfully
To play down any weaknesses.
Of weaknesses or fragility in Christy, I am
Unaware; any such, be intrinsic to our species,
And well contained, I surmise, from her
Childhood home and parentage so well
Adapted and restrained, root and foundation
Of her personality, firm and fair.
You need only see her handwriting, her
Personality written there.

Though impressively tall, for a lady, she
Commands attention not for this, but
From her confidence, her courtesy, her
Air of capability – soundly supplied of
These is she.
It is a cultural height from which she
Speaks; unforced and thoroughbred, it
Seems to me, from her patrician manner
To her polished vowels – genuine throughout.

A warm and loyal companion, Christy
Proved to be, of qualities against which
To measure oneself. More widely read,
I'd say, than anyone else I have met –
On any subject, bar the most technical
And arcane, she can converse, with such
A range of references, and with fine

Discretion. Add to this, gleanings and
Perspectives transatlantic, from a working
Lifetime in Massachusetts, and much
Travel in Western Europe.

Whenever it is said that laughter is the
Best medicine, one has to wonder at the
Sickness.
Genuine laughter, surely, is a helplessness,
An incontinent leaking-out of stress.
In my experience, Christy does not laugh.
To any witticism or joke, possibly a chuckle,
But a smile of intellectual recognition at
The essence of the joke.

To say that Christy does not need to laugh
Is to emphasise the point; pure laughter is
Passive, not active – something that finds
You out – no weakness this, in Christy, but
Strength. So robust is she of disposition, of
Psyche; if there be any stress within, it is
So disciplined, so well contained.

Nobody, of course, can be reduced to words on
A page, but let it be said that from Christy – home
Now, in her native Wales — and such in the world
As she, there are lines we may learn, about how
In this world we may cope. Without a trace of
Self-pity in her loss of mobility, Christy is wisdom,
Benevolence, good humour and hope.

PHILLIPS

In my mind it rose, the other day, as
Naturally as any bubble, rising from the
Depths of a pond; surfaced, popped open
To recall those few moments, sequestered
Somehow, seventy years or so, ago.

Chippenham Grammar School, Sports Day,
Nineteen fifty-one, or two, and Phillips
Had been entered for 'The Mile' – four
Times, in those days, around the four-forty
Yards athletics track.

In every year-group, in school, as we know,
Developmental rates of change begin to show;
Some boys to be taller, more muscular; others,
Like young Phillips, less so, or slower to grow.
Yet, on Sports Day, his House had put him
Forward to represent them, in 'The Mile'.

All I can remember about that race, is
That when a taller, stronger boy breasted
The finishing-tape, Phillips was weakening,
Half a lap behind. The runners-up soon
Finished, well before Phillips was even
In the home straight.

Though it was lost to me, for seventy years
Or so, I can see it vividly now.
The spectators, the rest of the school, lined
That finishing straight, for him, and as he
Passed them, closed in behind him, clapping
And cheering him on, until he completed
His Personal Mile, with such determination,
Across that finishing line.

I can recall, at that moment, a shiver of feeling,
A catching of breath, almost a tear — touched,
I now suppose, by some truth, something
Wonderful, and even sad, about our kind.

The vagaries of memory forever tease us:
Whatever the nature of this vellum, this
Tissue within us, upon which memories
Are inscribed, it may be this shivering of
Feeling, this catching of breath, stifling of
A tear, that adds a special sharpness, to
The quill. So that long afterwards, bubbles
Of memory may rise, for us to feel those
Moments still – goodness knows how, but
Partake so keenly of those moments, now.

HARRUMPH

Sometimes, it's the little things, you know,
That just catch at us and will not let us go.
Why it should so be, I'm not so sure, but
Little things do seem to matter to me.

Those four pieces, at the corners of your
Chess-board – do they look to you like
Rooks, or might they resemble castles?
Even if you were born and bred in a
Liberal-minded rookery, I doubt you
Would ever admit those castellated lumps
As honorary rooks.
Yet by masters and mistresses of chess,
Who should know better, as 'rooks' are
They stubbornly known.

Too often, are castles of correctness and
Plain good sense besieged; too often ramparts
Of reason and good taste overrun by
Visigoths and vandals.
Harrumph!

To let dumb solecisms pass us by, —
Unthinkable for sensitive souls, such
As I – as on Government Forms worded
With such limited sub-literacy: On the
Passport Renewal Form, the question
Was posed, 'Who is this Passport for?'
Wearily, in pencil I corrected it. There
Must be scope and room, in our education
System, to recognise once more, resurrect
And reinstate that handy pronoun, 'whom'.
Harrumph!

Wishing to reserve a table for two, for half-
Past six, I found I had to reserve it for
Eighteen-thirty, presumably to make clear
That I was not booking an early breakfast.
'Little things' like this are not little things
To me. Eighteen-thirty indeed: Pomposity,
Affectation, humbug.
Harrumph!

More recently, an on-line booking
Demanded to know the day and time
Of course, but also the 'amount' of
People. Amount? The quantity? The
Mass? Heap? How many cartloads?
How many hundredweight?
Perhaps they meant simply the 'number'
Of people: Literacy limited, all around us.
Harrumph!

Congratulations, Polly Ponsonby, on
Gaining your medical degree, but please
Madam, please do not keep telling me
That your name is Doctor Ponsonby.
More than likely, it is not.
Congratulations, Freddy Blenkinsop, on
Gaining the Chair of your Faculty, but
Please, sir, oh please do not keep telling me
That your name is Professor Blenkinsop.
More than likely, it is not.
Harrumph to the pair of you!

Such little things do catch at me; the
World seems other than it ought to be,
Tormenting sensitive souls.

Those calendars we hang on our kitchen
Walls – why would they prefer to shove
The thirtieth and thirty-first up before
The first of the month, rather than make
More space at the end? I'll tell you why;
It's just to irritate.

"Three times in as many days" is a neat-enough
Common phrase, how often now mangled by
The sub-literate "Third time in as many days".
How many days? Why, third days.
Harrumph!

Before you open your cornflakes packet, I bet
You store it in your cupboard with the lettering
The right way up. So do I, for pleasingly enough,
The bag inside only opens thus, at the top.

Unlike cornflake packets, those heavy-duty
Plastic sacks of top-soil or fertilizer, which
Come in handy later for all sorts of garden use,
Can be split for emptying, at either end.
For there is no obvious top or bottom.
Oh yes, there is! For There Is Lettering On Them!
Believe it or not, there be some philistines
In our midst who would slit open those sacks
So that forever after, those letters can only be
Read if you are standing on your head.
Harrumph!

Little things, you know, that catch at us,
And will not let us go.
A Hundred Times Harrumph!

PERSONIFY

To personify the Creator of All Things as
Our progenitor, Our Father, would seem to
Claim for ourselves a divinity which, looking
About us in the world, we scarcely deserve.
From such a blessed provenance, have we
Erred and strayed indeed.

To personify our Source, over evolutionary
Time, as Mother Nature, would seem to highlight
Ourselves as benefactor, choice inheritor, of
Earthly fortunes. Divinity or inheritor, what
Prodigal sons and daughters are we proving to be.

But to personify seems – seems, seems, always
It has to be 'seems' – to be the best we can do,
To comprehend ourselves, accommodate ourselves
As father, mother, daughters and sons; the best
That such a figure of speech sustains, such the
Restlessness in human veins.

CLOCK

Refurbishment was overdue, for this
Old family clock, but the void in her
Absence is so much wider than the
Space vacated, on top of the old oak
Bookcase.
About a century old is she, with a carved
Oak encasement of her own, having timed
And chimed the lives of my late wife, and
Her parents long before her.

My loyal companion she will always be,
So long as I am hers; all she asks of me is
Re-winding from time to time. If ever I
Forget to re-wind, the room positively pauses;
Her silence admonishes me.
With such dependable hands and such a wise
Old face, a loyal companion she surely will
Be, to whoever takes my place.

Just as our pulse is unnoticed, until we
Feel for it, so is the kik-kluk, kik-kluk
Unheard, unless we attend to it – so much
Does such a clock become a part of us.

Mechanism she may be, but in a sense,
Are not we? She gives structure to our days,
For the ordering of our days, but we cannot
Unhitch ourselves from Time – weeks, months,
Passing years, forever chiming, in our ears.

Mistress clock never sleeps at night, but keeps
Her vigil the whole night through; where else
Is such a friend?

Before too long may she return, restored and
Refreshed – resume her pride of place again,
On top of the bookcase once again, the household
Rendered whole again, and I with my dear old
Friend again.

WOODPIGEON

Poor thing, Susie;
You poor thing, Susie!
Just what is that nest, Susie?
Were you never taught to bind and
Weave a cosy bowl of mosses and hair
And grasses and leaves to cradle your
Eggs and your dovelets? Why just a
Flimsy platter of twigs?
You poor thing, Susie;
Poor thing, Susie, You.

'plicity, Cousin; simplicity, Cousin.
Why to bother to bind and weave, when
All they do is mess it up, and fledge and
Squawk and leave? They feed, they grow
And then they go; fancy nests are just for
Show: To give each egg my fullest care, I
Usually do no more than two, hoping to
Get a 'pigeon pair'
Simplicity, Cousin;
'plicity, Cousin, Sim.

Poor thing, Susie;
You poor thing, Susie!
Whatever is that song, Susie?
Where is melody, where is joy;
Whatever be you doing; what could be
Flatter than repetitive tuneless cooing?
You poor thing, Susie;
Poor thing, Susie, You.

'mility, Cousin; humility, Cousin.
Throughout the woods, this dawning
Chorus – a little too exuberant for us,
Rather more hope than expectation; we
Like to coo and croon a much more sober
Tune – and see how easily we birds, in our
Phrasing and our stressing, slip into those
Of the birds we're addressing.
As modest as our plumage, our message
More restraint than show, as true to pigeons
As coarseness to the magpie and the crow.
Humility, Cousin;
'mility, Cousin, Hu.

Poor thing, Susie;
You poor thing, Susie!
I declare, by our Great Feathered One
Above, I know not if you be pigeon, or
If you be dove: Address you, some, as
Woodpigeon; as Ring Dove, others do.
You poor thing, Susie;
Poor thing, Susie, You.

'cerity, Cousin; sincerity, Cousin.
For by my troth, we be something of both:
Pigeons, in truth, are we – Columba Palumbus,
If you really wish to know, which translates
Pretty well as 'Big Softies'. As pigeons we
Clap and flap, and power-fly and glide; as
Doves, our gentler, peaceful side.
We posture and strut, in plump and self-important
Manner. But don't be deceived by narrow
Heads; far from narrow-minded are we:
We think things out, you see. When we form
A mating pair, a mating pair for life are we –
Proudly known as 'monogamy'.

Sincerity, Cousin;
'cerity, Cousin, Sin.

   'give me, Susie;
Forgive me, Susie!
Not I to pity you, but you to pity me:
My cool friend, Susie –
My mild friend, Susie –
My open friend, Susie –
All natural, yes; compelling, yes
To be phrasing and stressing
As those whom we're addressing –
And so with you and all your kind,
Susie, such a blessing;
A blessing, Susie, Such.

LORD'S PRAYER

Anciently prescribed, and so 'biblified',
The Lord's Prayer was fed to us, as young
Children, staple part of our early spiritual
Nourishment. God was our Father in Heaven
And we had to pray to Him, every morning
At school, because He made us all, as well
As Heaven and Earth.

The word 'which', in the opening line, was
Chanted just as mindlessly as all the other
Words in our Morning Assemblies. In order
To pray, that was what people had to say.
Until now, many years later, I had never
Pondered that word 'which', accepting it,
I suppose, as denoting the Lord's supremacy,
As distinct from human kind.

But in recent years, egalitarians here and
There do not wish to be subordinated so,
By this word, insisting on changing 'which'
To 'who'.

A bit presumptuous at first sight –
Personal pronoun, for the Almighty –
And when we assign masculinity to Him,
We do at least use a capital H. To call
Him 'Father', moreover, does seem a bit
Familiar: It is the Creator of Heaven and
Earth, no less, with 'whom' we fraternise.

To some, it does seem a touch reverential
Though, to use 'which' – even demeaning.
But as soon as you instal the more matey
'Who', you crunch up against the archaic
Verb 'art'. 'Who art' sounds so clumsy to
Me – for a God whose name is to be 'Hallowed'.

And then to reduce 'thy' to 'your', and 'thine'
To 'yours', does seem to strip away another
Layer of respect, let alone worship.
'Yours' does sound too casual, a little too
Domestic.
Being made in God's image does not, I
Suspect, imply a replicating, a cloning –
More likely a cri-de-coeur in human vanity.
If each person is merely a clone, who needs
God? You or I can stand alone.

Even from my atheistic point of view, I
Would wish upon Believers the elegance
Of traditional wording. Otherwise, the
Vernacular seeds will take root:

"Mornin' Gov'ner, some place out there:
Live up to y'name and sort out this mess
Down 'ere. Just give us what's good for
Us Gov, and turn a blind eye to – y'know –
Things we give a nod and wink to down 'ere.
Please don't make us any worse than we are,
Gov. Keep us on the right road, if y'know
What I mean. It's your show, after all. Cheers."

NOUGHT

The Diabetic-Eye-Screening Van was in
The local car-park that morning – a facility
New, to save patients having to travel to
Gloucester every year.

Having covered up one eye, and then the
Other, to read out the smallest row of letters
On the wall-chart, I was then given the
Eye-drops. Back to the waiting area then,
For my pupils to dilate, while the next in the
Queue, a smiling Scottish lady, took my place.
Waiting there, through the thin partition
I could clearly hear the lady, responding as
Best she could, to the wall-chart:
"W – S – Y" What? Did she say Zero? Yes,
A little later, "B – X – T – Zero". No figures
On these charts; she was reading the letter O !
Delightful surprise – upon the routine testing
Of the eyes.
When she came out, for dilating, I briefly shared
My amusement with her: A Scottish thing, maybe.
It should have been no surprise: How
Long in this country have we been lazily
Misnaming the figure Nought, or Zero,
As a sound like the letter O ?
Irretrievably, within my lifetime, it has
Entered the language.
In my earlier, stricter days, the figure Zero
Always was spoken of as Nought. One

Tenth was Nought point One; one hundredth,
Nought point Nought One. Greenwich is
On Nought degrees of longitude.
But hanker as I may, for the old-time Nought,
Ask me for my area-code, and I'll answer
With the rest, 'Oh', One, Nine, Eight, Nine.
It has an appealing slickness about it,
I suppose, replacing clumsy Noughts by 'Oh's —
(James Bond, as Agent Nought Nought Seven,
Not so deadly, I suppose.)

A certain logic, I can see: If Nought can be a
Simple 'Oh', why not the letter O a Zero?
A happy alphabet amendment may it be –
J K L M N ZERO P Q R S T.

MASK

It was a night well slept, I could tell, for
The time had passed without me; less had
I slept, than I had been slept. No more
Had I woken, than been awakened, and
Released.

No more might be said of any of us, I dare
Say; of what overnight mind meanderings
There may have been, few made known
To us – scarcely a whisper of dream recalled –
The sleep of infancy, vulnerable, unaware.

Day composure sloughing off, involuntarily,
Under the covers, where no one may see –
Persona slipping and sagging from the mask –
As if we had been someone, or something,
Other than we had appeared to be.

BERNARD KEAR

I try to imagine our descendants, centuries
Hence, watching, as moving History, recordings
Of our times here and now, such as the funeral
Of Queen Elizabeth the Second. I try to imagine
How moving History would have seemed if,
Here and now, the funeral of Elizabeth the First
Were available to us, similarly archived and screened.
For however full our research and our readings
Of days gone by, nothing can replace the witness
Of the human eye.
For all the Histories of Monarchs, governments,
Crises and wars, how might we know the daily
Lifetimes, the personal domestic lives, such as
Mine and such as yours? One sure way is through
The insights and the talents of sensitive souls
Such as Bernard Kear.
A good friend's good friend loaned me two
Published sketch-books of his, entitled 'Scenes
From Childhood', in which with consummate
Deftness he revealed his own childhood in the
Forest of Dean, during the Second World War.

Those being my own formative years too,
How could I not be moved?
Published some fifty years later, these
Wonderfully observed drawings depict
His own early days as one of a large family,
Five boys, three girls and their father, after
Their mother had died, in 1940.

A kind of moving History this surely is,
Archived in the memory, brought before us
By the human eye; too easy it is to romanticise,
Without the evidence of human eyes.

With such poignancy and yet with such pride
Does he sketch for us that two-bed cottage,
No electricity, no water supply: The endless
Chores as the months go by, subsistence growing
Of 'taters' and greens and beans; gathering of
Firewood; keeping hens; slaughtering the pig;
Cider pressing – the observance of Sundays –
Mischief and games, winter evenings, and
Christmas morning, when such meagre presents
Are opened with pure delight.

What is it, to be 'moved', to be so touched
As to have deep feelings stirred? I see myself
In the sketches of those boys – short trousers
And braces, sagging socks, short, scruffy hair.
I see such girls as I remember – all in simple
Dresses, hair held off the face with bows of tape,
Playing hopscotch, playing 'houses'.
In both senses, the artist 'draws' attention to
A girlishness so shaped and limited by those
Times. In his side-notes, he describes his sisters
As 'aspiring mothers', doing 'a lot of knitting,
Needlework and playing with dolls' while
'Developing their motherly instincts'.

For notwithstanding infant mortality, people
Then had large families – my own father was
One of eleven.
While girls now, are much freer to express
Themselves in other than domestic ways, the
Prospects of motherhood for those Kear girls
Were unrelenting, and exhausting.

Every one of his evocative sketches is
Enriched by a snatch of the Forest Patois,
Uttered by one of those portrayed:
"I sh'ink y' be got there mind. Ketch olt on'n
An' screw thic there doin's on'n" – a pattern
Of speech echoing my own post-war days in
Wiltshire. The only difference is Bernard Kear's
Gentle bowdlerising: Along with tyke, blighter
And mugwump, 'sod' is the strongest, compared
With rougher words of my recalling.

A mere moment of human History we have,
Chronicled, illuminated for us here, a brief
Distilling and essence of passing time, and the
Passing of those brief lives in the nineteen-forties,
In the Forest of Dean.

Thank you, Bernard Kear, for this generous
Offering. I suspect your drawings will leave a
Deeper mark on human minds than many
Histories of Kings and Queens.
Rest in peace.

BRECON CANAL

Funny how hopes, and even expectations,
Run away with the mind, even after all the
Lessons of the years – but there was I, booking
A narrow-boat holiday in a Wind-in-the-Willows,
April Springtime frame of mind, mellow Dawn-
Choruses in my ears. Reality, instead, soon dawned.

When your hands are on the tiller, there is no
Time to stand and stare. Following the contour,
As it must, the waterway twists and bends,
Spanned by numerous bridges, underneath which
A narrow-boat must be narrowly threaded; no
Time to stand and stare. And springtime that year,
Was retarded, sunlight intermittent, with a gusty,
Penetrating breeze – and furthermore, the canal itself,
The central attraction, fell short. Wide enough, to
Serve its commercial purpose, but navigable now,
Only if kept clear by routine dredging which, so
Evidently, had been neglected; navigable now, only
If you keep to the middle, and even there sometimes not,
With the boat scraping the silted bed.

Mooring places, consequently, far apart.
Neglect unmistakeable, all along, in the
Drifts of flotsam from the overhanging trees –
Not only twigs and leaves, but the occasional
Log-sized branch.

Ah, those overhanging trees, those Weeping
Willows which follow and grace our waterways.
Standing at the tiller, you have to duck from
Time to time to avoid them, and fend them off,
Harmless enough, even pleasing.
But what if you were wearing spare socks, as
Gloves, against that chilly breeze? What if you
Were sporting your new yachting-cap to look
The part as a seasoned mariner? And what if,
Dangling unnoticed among those willow fronds,
Were several thorny briars – yes, thorny briars,
At that height – why, your cap might be hooked
Off your head as you ducked, and scratches torn
In the back of your jacket? Then might you glance
Back to see your new cap floating and sinking, and
A left-handed sock suspended above the canal.

Then might those Weeping Willows be
Heard, bursting and weepingly weak with
Laughing at what they had seen – or was
That my merry First Mate, by the name of
Jean?
And then, the 'decapitated', even I, could see
The comical side of it.
For what the hell – of such moments are
Memories made, and tales to tell.
People and good humour prevailed, as
Always they must: For all our disappointments,
It was the people we met who came out winners.
Among the Beacon Park staff, strollers on the
Towpath, or other boaters, there was a palpable
Fellowship, and an ever-readiness to help.

On our return leg, what is more, who should
Retrieve my left-handed sock, but the undisputed
Canal-boat Queen, my thoroughly good companion,
Jean.

EMBODIMENT

How it pleases me to see this old land of
Ours, so personified – Britain as Britannia,
Confidently at ease, clutching Neptune's
Trident, with helmet and with shield. It is
Her womanhood, not these; essence of our
Country, embodied in the female form: We
Neither threaten, nor shall we yield.

How it pleases me to see our fundamental,
Crucial virtue, Justice, so personified: The
Very soul of fairness, she tempers judgement
With mercy, weighing evidence in her scales.
It is her womanhood – essence of Justice,
Embodied in the female form more completely
Than the male's.

How it pleases me to see our precious human
Liberties – civil, political, religious, so personified
In womanhood, in New York Harbour.

Custodian and guarantor, she towers proudly
As a welcome, holding aloft that everlasting
Torch of Freedom – essence of Liberty – so
Embodied in the female form.

So might other fine qualities and virtues, within
Our kind, be honoured and embodied, with
Provenances in myth, in faith, in sculpture, from
Ancient days. How it pleases me, in this Man's
World, to see such praise in our traditions and
In our Art, for womanhood.

GRATUITY

On their last emptying of the bins –
Landfill and recycling bins – before
Christmas each year, I leave a 'tip'
For the waste-disposal lads.
As grateful as they are to receive it,
I imagine, am I so pleased each year,
To give it.
Contrasted with other forms of 'tipping',
It has a simpleness and virtue – it is
Neither hinted at nor, I like to think,
Routinely expected.
Recognising the tedious nature of this
Essential work, it is my wish each year
To reward it so.
Sad to recognise, therefore, that tipping
The taxi-driver, the waiter, the porter, has
Lost its simpleness and virtue.
If a tip fulfils an expectation, it has lost
Its innocence, lost its purity, rather lost
Its point – more a surcharge than a reward.

The gesture is so devalued when
Restaurants prompt the option of
A tip. Restaurateurs do but embarrass
Customers and demean themselves –
More likely to be tipped, I should guess,
If they had not prompted. Let the
Troubled conscience be with the one who
Expects a tip, not the one who may disburse it.

Is a bare minimum of efficiency expected
In return for wages? A perverse world
Would this be, but such is implied if tips
Are given simply for efficient service –
No more should long and loyal civil service
Expect a knighthood or a peerage.

Let there be no whiff of bribery around
Gratuity. May recipients be surprised
And be delighted.
Let us reclaim the simple virtue of the tip –
Voluntary, spontaneous, unexpected, for
Exceptional personal service.

TREE

They have little to say, do the trees, but
We mustn't hold that against them; some
People say little, but so prove their worth
In the service they provide, in the examples
They set, for us all.
They have little to say, do the trees, but
Pass on rumours from the breeze.
Deciduous or evergreen, with such strength
Of character and forbearance, such example
Do they set, bearing silent witness to us all.

No habitable world to be imagined, without
Trees, established long before us here, as it
Were to set the stage, that we may marvel at
Their permanence, their age; everlastingly
In awe, of trees.
In every joist and beam, in every plank and
Rafter, how we honour our trees, braced
Against come what may; with all our tables
And chairs, cabinets, shelves and stairs,
Furnishing ours from what was theirs.

Odd way to worship, this would seem to
Be, but if we need to worship, what better
Than worship Tree: Justly venerated trades,
Are carpentry and joinery.

Who can be indifferent to a tree? For in their
Image, so arranged and bound are we; from
Trunk roads to local branches, analogies abound.
Lineage, roots and branches, sketched out as
Our personal family trees.

They have little to say, do the trees.
Deciduous or evergreen, so dependable are
Trees – such towering fountains of life and
Shade, sustaining, accommodating, teeming
Forms of life.
What example, what a presence, is a tree.
Such patient power, so grounded; a grasp on
Life to be envied: Just look at the spreading,
Muscular knuckles of their roots, reaching,
Delving and clamping to this living earth.
Little to say, have the trees, but so much to teach.

PROTTY

From these unfathomable depths of
Memory, up bubbled another recently,
Some seventy years after it had been,
Unwittingly, stored away.
I followed in those early days, an interest
In 'Nature', as we called it. Casual or
Incidental to whatever has ruled my grown-
Up years, the natural world around me
Would always draw my gaze.
The memory popped the other day, on my
Lifting a stone, in the garden, as the woodlice
Scuttled away to safety.

At a similar moment, seventy years before –
I would be about twelve – Roy, from along
The lane, referred to the woodlice as 'protty-dogs',
An odd name which meant nothing to me at
The time; I have always been, as people used
To say 'slow on the uptake'.

Roy's understanding of religion, I guess,
Was even less than mine. Then aged about
Nine, he had evidently caught the term
'Protty-dogs' from his parents – Irish Roman
Catholics, both.

All Protestants, it was clear, were equated
To crawling, nocturnal crustaceans, with
Seven pairs of legs, to be found in decaying
Wood, or under stones – one brief glimpse of
Inter-faith contempt –
Hawthorn, Wiltshire, circa Nineteen-Fifty.

SKY

This Sky of ours is not defined by
Any but our questing human mind –
Not quite molecular, as the elements
In the air, which we may breathe, nor
Water-vapour, which we may measure,
But something lacking substance.

I imagine there is no Sky, beyond the
Perception of the human eye, without a
Trepidation in the human mind.
It's what we wish upon ourselves, is our
Sky; what skies, we may ponder, are
Perceived in other creatures' eyes.

Having no more substance than the Time,
Or the Date, the Sky has become necessary,
More real, a natural context, a coverlet,
Drawn up against unknowable void, a
Faculty of foreboding born.

Even the Sky at Night, for all its
Mystery and vastness, is familiarised,
Given humanising names, enlisted as
Keeping everlasting vigil over us.

Nor can I help feeling that this Sky of
Ours, in its provenance, is far from being
Our only child – that the entire pantheon
Of our Gods, incorporeal as our Sky, is in
This same womb conceived. Human awareness,
Might it not be, less a blessing than a
Curse, spreading fear, foreboding, of
Unknowable darkness and void.

Well might people pray, to keep dark
Nights, dark thoughts, at bay – and well
Might we draw comfort from a clear and
Cloudless summer Sky.

MORALITY

For communities to thrive, a morality is
Called for, a sense of what is right and what
Is wrong – a morality hand-in-glove with
Good manners – for as numbered are the
People, so many are their points of view,
That only overriding guidance, overriding
Rules, acceptable to most of us, will do.

And when I think back, in my humanistic
Way, over my snakes-and-ladders life, I have
To admit, and recognise, that the overriding
Guidance, the pervading moral force, in my
Dear Old England, was Christianity.
My early days were long on discipline, short
On warmth and personality; father supplied
The discipline, mother the rest as best she could,
Passing on a way of seeing things she herself
Had imbibed, with little understanding.
Being good meant doing as you were told,
While saying very little, a sense of conformity
And duty: Unlike father, mother was a Believer.

And so it was, implicit in my early years,
That the only way to moral health was the
Christian way.

Every morning, in School Assembly, we were
Obliged to sing a hymn, and say our prayers.
In retrospect, it was no more than routine, with
Little devoutness or faith about it, though I'm
Sure it reinforced a sense of School community.

Similarly, at Scout meetings, we promised to
"do our duty to God and the King" – the nature
Of our "duty" never made clear, always implied.
Looking back, I'm sure it was a similar binding
Thread in our moral education, and guide.

Most striking of all, in retrospect, were the Sunday
Morning services in Hartham parish church.
Along with the other choirboys, I turned to face
The altar. With serious, holy faces, we recited, in
Pre-pubescent voices, the Apostle's Creed, declaring
Beliefs far beyond our comprehension.

Re-reading the Apostle's Creed now, from
My humanistic point of view, I'm reminded
What a fundamental utterance it is, the
Purest Article of Christian faith.

However much I owe to, and am I grateful for,
The Christian faith, in our country, I need not
The supernatural, but the common-sense and
The reasonable, from which to find my bearings
In right and wrong.

Faith may embrace the virtues, but surely does
Not own them. Though somewhat lifted out of
Context, Matthew Chapter Seven would seem
To point to a rational way of forming morality:
"Whatsoever ye would, that men should do to
You, do ye even so to them", seeming to point to
A mutual, earthbound way to right and wrong.

So while the faithful draw their comfort from on
High, communities their overriding Rules thereby,
A similar comfort may we find, in the fellow-feeling,
Honesty and graciousness within our human kind.

CLOUD

They may not be aware, our fellow
Voyagers, our clouds, of this everlasting
Fellowship we share – even though from
Time to time, on more inquisitive days,
They do seem to lower their gaze, with
A grey and chilly Stratus cloud alighting
On the ground, enfolding us all within
Its haze, as if to sense that hereabouts,
Kinfolk may be found.

Indeed, no more are clouds today the
Very clouds of yesterday, than you or I
Are those who've gone before us: As passers-by
They share our fate, being but to dissipate.

Our clouds, stealing over chiefly from our
West, subject to depression, sunlight or
Prevailing winds, welcome or unwelcome
Guests, would seem to be our mirrors in the sky.

Rarely a day goes by, but upwards and
To our West, we'll consult our local clouds.
We'll see the looming rain-clouds, and
Declare it to be a miserable day, so tellingly
Are we within their sway.

We'll recognise the restlessness inherent in
Cumulus clouds, piling and puffing up with pride.

We'll understand those wisps of Cirrus, way up
High, icy, so remote from common things below.

We may welcome a blue and cloudless day, but
Hope for clouds at night, to keep the frosts at bay.

More than a passing acquaintance, all this; such
Weaving of cloudy and human affairs.
Be they the clouds of our imagination, or we but
Instruments of theirs?

MAKE-UP

Not even pretending to be something
Other than artifice – the very term 'make-up'
Just brazens it out, a contrivance, cover-up,
A deceit, in the name of something carelessly
Known as Beauty: Of its own irony, it does
Seem carelessly unconcerned.

Once, in a florist's corner shop, I noticed
Bouquets of flowers sprayed with a silvery
Glitter. 'Gilding the lily' was the phrase I had
In mind, imperfectly remembered or misquoted,
I now know, from Shakespeare's King John:
  "To gild refined gold, to paint the lily,
    To throw a perfume on the violet"

Was not the flower lovely enough, said I –
Like a beautiful lady applying make-up to
Her face? To which a reply, along the lines –
Beauty being beauty, why not beauty more?

Divided as we are, female from the male,
Inherent in our nature for one to advertise,
Appealing to the other's seeking eyes.
As the Bard himself implied, the lily, the
Violet, perfect in themselves, we never need
Enhance. But out here, in the human sphere,
It's as plain to the seeker, as to the sought –
Make-up is disguise.

So far satisfying, if we are to peer no deeper
Than the skin, but there's mischief in the
Superficial, if at odds with what there lies within.
So we others had better look the advertisers
In the eye, to fathom if a deeper kind of beauty
There within may lie – a gracious heart, an
Unaffected charm.

And so I'm back where I began, I guess: Lipsticks,
Creams and powders, mascaras, perfumes all, as
Make-up do themselves confess.
I'm back where I began: The made-up lady not
Deceitful, but plainly honest to her man.

TRAFFIC

You get a better view, when you are
Seated in a touring coach, a step or two
Higher than in your car, and not driving;
You're freer to notice, and to contemplate,
Especially to witness from this vantage
Point, the restlessness of the road – a
Traffic river in full spate.

Organic, so it seems, two-lane or three-lane
Highways, outward bound or inward bound;
Traffic-bound – urgency in circulation.
Organisms ourselves, in thrall to organism
Greater still. The analogy is unavoidable –
Throughout our waking hours, traffic coursing
Through the country's arteries and veins.
If this were the lifeblood of a nation, the
Nation would never sleep; the analogy falters.
But if this be the haste in a nation's heart,
What so possesses its mind?
Just what phantom foxes do these Traffic-
Hounds pursue?

Some chronic emptiness, it must be,
Some insufficiency to be filled, whichever
Way we turn; as we are driven, so must
We drive. In this age of communication,
Instant and worldwide, why this headlong
Haste? Just where is everybody bound –
And why whatever sought, so seldom found?

Fulfilment, even survival, lies elsewhere, it
Would appear. A state of sufficiency lies
Elsewhere, never here: As if to tease us,
Elsewhere, it lies.

Small cars, large cars, vans of every size –
Trucks and trailers, caravans in tow – tankers,
Articulated lorries, join the flow – with here
And there excursion coaches for the likes
Of me and you, to witness in amazement
From our lofty point of view.

FRAGMENTS

One irritating consequence of surrendering
Our British ways, to ways European, is that
The kitchen oven clock knows nothing of 'am'
Or 'pm', but tells me that Two o'clock in the
Afternoon is One, Four, Zero, Zero – lest I should
Think it's Two in the morning.

Evening after evening, therefore, I'm reminded
Of key dates in my lifetime, from Nineteen
Thirty-seven (birth year) onwards, up to the age
Of Twenty-two in Nineteen fifty-nine.
It picks me up again at Eight o'clock pm, at the
Age of Sixty-three, thence to the time of writing
In Twenty twenty-four: Some reminders are
Welcome; others less so.

A moment ago, I saw Nineteen forty-six, a year
After the War ended, when I was sent to Corsham
Council School.

In a cautious approach to co-education,
There were separate playgrounds for girls
And boys, though at times this arrangement
Was relaxed. My memory is hazy, but I recall
Embarrassments at that age – girls keeping
To themselves, with hopscotch and skipping-
Ropes; the boys rowdier, often kicking a ball
Around, a rank order of juvenile toughness
Tacitly understood.

Memories beget memories: The other day,
I heard two primary-school girls chatting
About games at school, and was delighted
To find that so many years after my time,
Groups of children 'dipped' to decide who
Should start the game.
Pretty much the same as back then, when we
Dipped to find who would be 'on it', in a
Game of Tag – so, nowadays they still form
A circle, holding out a fist for "One potato,
Two potato, three potato four, five potato,
Six potato, seven potato more."

Some dips pointed to a winner, or loser,
In one go, others eliminated people one
At a time. I can recall only fragments of
Others – "Lady, baby, gypsy, queen..."
They were all rhythmic and ritualistic:
"This year, next year, sometime, never..."
I do remember one quite clearly, from a
Girl who came from Leeds, because of her
Bizarre incantation, "Eeny-meeny makarraka,
Rair rye dominakka, chikka-pakka, lolly-
Poppa pom pom pyneze push!"
With that mystical power, you were authorised
To start the game.
One of the commonest dips, I hardly dare
Point out, began and ended with "Eeny-meeny
Miny mo" – innocent enough, I suppose, back
Then, but out of the question now, even as
A playground 'dip'.

A moment ago, I saw Nineteen fifty-three,
The year when, at the age of not-quite-sixteen,
I joined the Navy – a fast farewell to 'civvy-street'.

Measured up, were we, on Day One,
Issued with uniforms, caps, socks, boots
And shoes; holdall, kitbag and gasmask.
One item issued was a roll-up cloth wallet
Containing needles and thread and spare
Buttons. What a sign of those days, that
It was listed in Naval stores as 'One Housewife.'

Baptised were we, from Day One, as 'sprogs'
In a font of jargon, limited, in basic training,
To a novice paddle in the shallows of jargon,
Prior to surfing the salty seas of Naval slang.
As with all jargon, in trades and professions,
It was a badge of membership, a kind of
Exclusion zone inside the moat and the keep:
The toilets were 'Heads', your best pal was
Your 'Oppo', refuse was 'Gash', cigarettes
Were 'Burns', your uniform was your 'Rig',
Your cap, your 'Goss'; you filled in a 'slop-chit'
To buy items from 'Slops', the cash clothing
Store;

You did not go to bed, you 'Turned in';
You 'Turned out' in the morning; you didn't
Wash your pants and socks, you 'Dhobeyed'
Them – washing-powder was 'Dhobey dust'.

Memories beget memories of jargon: Once, a
Fellow building a wall for me, said, of the transverse
Coping-stones, "They're what we call Toppers."

Having had a growth removed from my ear,
I learned that these outer flaps are known as
'Pinnas' – and I wonder whether in the medical
World, 'Gravid' means anything other than 'pregnant.'

PARA BELLUM

Each time something 'moves' us, stirs
Our feelings, we learn or affirm a little
More about ourselves.
By today's Trooping of the Colours was
I so moved – unsurprisingly for me, a
Patriot, formerly of the Royal Navy,
Watching this great display of drill in
Precision, regiments proudly bearing
Battle honours embroidered on their Colours.

An unavoidable truth it is, a sad indictment
Of mankind, that if you want Peace, you
Had better prepare for War.
Such parades as these, serve to remind us
That there are ways of life worth fighting
For, even dying for.

The whole event is a public act of loyalty,
By the Armed Forces, to the Sovereign –
Total dedication of service to the Crown,
And the great Cause it symbolises.

It has to be a matter of symbolism:
The Sovereign – himself in military
Uniform – takes the salute, standing
As living embodiment of our Nationhood,
Inheritor, and custodian, of essential
Human qualities which can only be
Expressed as abstract nouns, such as
Peace, justice and honour – within which
A human society may thrive.

Though ours is a 'Constitutional Monarchy',
Detached from political matters, the principle
Simply devolves upon those who legislate
In his name.

So without being 'warlike', by all means let
Us prepare for War, evermore, to guarantee
For generations to come such 'unalienable rights'
As expressed by Thomas Jefferson – 'Life, Liberty,
And the pursuit of Happiness'.

INSEPARABLE

So often, it's a thought of what I might
Have said at the time, had I more confidence
And a sharper mind.

Lunch parties these days, hereabouts,
Serve a purpose other than for keeping
Ourselves alive. There is a kind of security
About them, drawing people together,
Pooling views on matters great and small,
Lamenting the latest News, and the state
Of this modern world.

Only yesterday, at one point, the hostess
Opined that Religion gave rise to most of
The ills of this world – to which a guest
Replied, the problems were not Religions
Themselves, but those who claim to act
In the name of Religion: It's People, not Religion.

Only today, on reflection, can I suggest
What I might have said, to that guest.

Religion, and People – inseparable, not far
From synonymous, surely. How can you have
One without the other? In the absence of
Humankind, what possible Religion could
There be?

What Beliefs, without believers?

What Faiths, without the faithful?

What Gods, without worshippers?

We might as well seek to separate the
Dancer from the Dance,
The Dreamer from the Dream.

DIALOGUE

One set of assumptions I had imbibed
From my early days, concerned the
Character of British people – English
Particularly, but British as a whole.
Britain, the British, stood for moral
Uprightness, a pride in their country,
And all the virtues it has bestowed upon
The world: The British are courteous,
Truthful, honourable, with an inborn
Sense of fairness. An Englishman's
Word is his bond.

Against that unblemished background,
However conceived, therefore, do stains
And smudges show up ever the more –
As here, in this pre-election campaign, in
The summer of Twenty-twenty-four.
Much like the verbal slanging-match that
Is 'Prime Minister's Questions' in the
House, ad hominem insults, if only implied,
Are the order of the day.

As feckless deceivers are political
Opponents routinely dismissed, their
Policies scorned, characters shamelessly
Traduced; opponents less likely to be
Respected than held in contempt – thus
Is our national discourse so degraded.
All those assumptions about the British,
The English – were they built on sand?

Listening in, today, so are we reminded
Of MP's expenses scandals, cash-for-questions,
Business interests undeclared, confidences
Betrayed, 'partygate', the calculated freezing-
Out of a Prime Minister – yes, a Prime Minister —
In Forty-nine days, by petulant colleagues in
Parliament, and now, at the time of writing,
Insider-betting on the General Election date.
We can but reflect on humankind: From which
Dark seams are such amoralities mined?

It should not be so difficult to find representatives,
Leaders, journalists even, with a modicum of
Self-restraint, even a sense of courtesy.

In place of constructive dialogue, discourteous
Diatribe is what we witness, infected throughout
By the plague of modern politics – opponents
'Talking Over' one another:
The principle is elementary, and benign: Just as
You wish to be heard, without interruption, you
Must never interrupt others.

Is this too much for you to grasp?

THE EYES

For all the arts and crafts of
Humankind, there can be no
Suborning of the eyes, to falsify
The mind. Stubbornly authentic
Are the eyes: From the coldness
Of the psychopath, to the warmth
And fondness of the lover, authentic
Are the eyes.

No such loyalty in our lips, or not
Necessarily so – for facial language
At the lips can dissemble; lips may
Counterfeit. Lips may appear to smile,
But tell rather of suspicion, or of doubt.

Furthermore, there is, inherited in so
Many human faces a certain composure,
Fixity, a certain restraint, where even
The most genuine smile sits ill-at-ease,
Whatever amusement or goodwill may
Be in the mind.

We have two examples before us,
In our new Queen, and indeed our
New Prince of Wales – both no doubt
Good-humoured and warm-hearted
People, but not quite able to smile.

No — for the Truth we must rely
Only upon the eyes, hardly capable,
It seems to me, of lies. While of course
A smiling face is often open and true,
It's always worth attending to the
Eyes, for a dependable point of view.

SCAPEGOAT

Our United Kingdom economy, our
Nationwide production and distribution
Of goods and services, comprises such
A complex of human activities in factories,
Companies, government local and central,
Customers, insurers, speculators, traders,
Banks, transport, taxes, supply and demand,
And so much more.
Well, Liz Truss crashed it all. Yes, believe it
Or not, Liz Truss "Crashed the Economy".

Which gifted idiot it was, who coined this
Phrase, I know not, but must surely be awarded
This year's Nobel Prize for the silliest and
Most pernicious glibness.
For it has been seized upon by so many flashy
Parrots in our jungle, puffing themselves up
With this neatly packaged nonsense, as if it
Were deep wisdom.

How unquestioningly do people yield to
Dim-witted orthodoxies, and parrot them devoutly,
As if to baptise themselves into the Faith:
"Liz Truss crashed the economy".

Repeat it often enough and knowingly enough:
It is as good as Gospel. For is that not the function
Of a Scapegoat? Let us lay upon Liz Truss all
The iniquities of the Children of Israel, and
Release her into the Wilderness, that we may
All be cleansed of our sins.

However ill-advised, the mini-budget drawn up
By Liz and her Chancellor, it was far, far, from
The 'crashing' of the British economy — but in the
Nostrils of supporters of her rival, it must have
Had a stench about it of 'just the pretext they were
Waiting for'.
All support for her, they withdrew – that she
Was obliged to go to the Palace, in effect to request
Banishment, into the political wilderness.

This was a day of shame, I would say, not
So much for Liz Truss, but for the moral health
Of this 'United' Kingdom.

Let us hold back from demonising this good
Lady, in order to promote ourselves. Let us
Not consign this good lady to the fate of the
Late Enoch Powell, similarly scapegoated,
Even now, in his grave.
Was he not a nasty racist?
Well, since you ask, no, he was not. He was
A courteous, open-minded patriot, as perceptive
And conscientious a public servant as this
Country has ever known: Please read his biography.

Did he not say there would be rivers of blood?
Well, since you ask, no, he did not: Please read
That 'incendiary' speech.

Yet everlastingly traduced, is that great man, if
Not in the annals of our great nation, then in
Generations following, who would sooner hitch
Their minds to pious orthodoxies, rather than
Think for themselves, and search for the truth.

Let us preserve Liz Truss, and all of her kind,
From such an ignominious fate.

DULLARD

I recall, in some of those early comics
I read, there would be a silly-looking
Boy – always a boy – in the corner of the
Class, with a conical cap upon his head.
He was the classroom Dunce,
(Before we had A4 paper, there was a size
Of paper known as 'Foolscap', for it bore
A watermark in the shape of a Dunce's cap.)
I seem to be descended from him, for ever
Since that elementary stage, I've needed
Things explained to me again, more than once.
At the secondary stage, it was evident even more,
As dumbly listening to the brighter ones, after
Each exam: What did you get for Question Four?
However willingly in life we play our part,
We can play only these cards we have been dealt:
If our Spades outweigh our Diamonds, our
Clubs outnumber our Hearts, we may be
Resigned, in the Acts and Scenes of life, to
Playing supporting parts – short-suited as
We are, in personality, and self-confidence.

As to its origins, its tributaries, in nature
And nurture, we may hazard a guess.
In my home, neither parent was educated;
Emotionally limited, both; so little range of
Thought or discourse, semi-detached from
Their children. Whatever more there was,
Than this, to try to account for my dullness,

Does not relieve me from my distress, my
Lifelong, embarrassing slow-wittedness.

So impressionable are young minds; we must
Be aware of what we are imprinting there.
In our classrooms, over and above the teaching
Of particular subjects, must be every teacher's
Concern, 'in loco parentis', for the development
Of the child, the encouragement of confidence,
Courtesy, and personal responsibility.

Two memories of the opposite – discouragement –
Occur to me now, as I write. In my first school,
I had learned how to join letters together, to form
Words.

Transferred to a new school, I found that
They still wrote in isolated letters. "Please Miss",
I said, "I do double-writing".
"Is that what you call that rubbish?" she
Retorted, looking down from her perch, on
The edge of the Teacher's table. Her words
Remain with me, eighty years on.
Later, in secondary school, a bright lad read
Out his essay to the class. I put up my hand
And asked, "Sir, what does 'distorted' mean?"
I remember only that in his reply was a
Disappointment that I should be unaware of
Words my classmates were using.

Fairly well educated now, I remain a Dullard
In my slow-wittedness: And self-confidence was
Never in my playing-cards.
As a pupil, I rarely had the courage to raise a
Question in class, for fear of making so public
My ignorance.

Years later, as a Teacher myself, I was
Naturally aware of the duller pupil, with
Little to say; and something more occurred
To me: He – it was usually a boy — was not
Alone in his slowness to grasp.
My technique then was simple, and effective.
When pupil A asked a question, I would
Assume that he was alone in his confusion.
So I pointed to pupil B, to provide the answer.
When pupil B baulked, I would try pupil C,
And so on.
The revelation was, of course, that when a
Pupil asked a question, several others in the
Class were glad that he did so.
A further revelation often, was that I must
Brush up my teaching.
Lessons learned all round.

PETS

In our evolution from the 'darkness'
Of our ancestry, into this light – if this
Be light — we brought along some others
To serve us and sustain us.
Over millennia we domesticated them,
Weaned them from the wild, some for
Easier food, others to work for us, or to
Clothe us, cover us, against the cold and,
I imagine, against a new self-consciousness.

Still others, we gradually brought along to
Amuse us, in a way to flatter us, I suppose,
And ultimately as 'pets', to sustain us in a
Different way, as companions – as if to retain
Something of wild heritage; as if we felt in
Some strange way isolated, friendless.
It is one of the ironies of modern life, that in
Vast and growing populations there is so
Much loneliness, and such want of physical
Touch, revealed in this word 'pets'.

And so we pat and fondle and stroke
Our dogs, who are 'members of the family'
Now – these days given human names
Rather than the 'doggie' names of yesteryear.

We also shape and re-design them, if you
Please, through selective breeding, to our
Fashions and requirements. Something
Beyond pet ownership, they become as our
Accessories. But these are accessories which
Defecate. If those droppings fall within the
Boundary-fence of the owner's property,
Well and good, so far tolerable; if not, simply
Intolerable, anti-social, unacceptable.
At my present address, as in previous ones,
Neighbourhood cats, other people's pets,
Use my garden as their latrine.
At certain times of the year, moreover,
They become – well, you know, a bit excited,
Restless and messy. The kindest thing is to
Have them 'neutered' – for our convenience,
If not for theirs – a love of animals thus with
Limitations.
What more, is a neutered pet, than
A companionable, living toy?

Perceptive readers will infer that I take a
Dim view of all of this: Up to a point, I do.
But in all of the natural world, and our
Place within it, I have a lifelong interest.
With the plight of mankind, as I perceive it,
I am much concerned, or I would not be
Writing.
It is touching to see the loyalty of a well-kept
Dog, to its master, and the mutual affection
Between the two – while a touch sad also,

That each should feel that need.
Without close reference to the keeping of
Pets, any social history of mankind will be
Incomplete.

While pet shops cater for all kinds, hamsters,
Guinea-pigs, rabbits, tortoises, cagebirds —
Even snakes, and stick-insects, stretching the
Meaning of 'pet' – these are fringe interests,
Beside the dog and the cat.

For there is nothing superficial about
The mutuality. The death of a family
Cat or dog can be wrenching to the
Bereaved owners, I can clearly see.
And we cannot forget the devotion of
Wee Bobby, that Skye terrier which –
Surely 'who' – stayed by his master's
Grave in Greyfriars kirkyard for fourteen
Years, no less, until the dog himself died,
To be buried nearby.
Pet ownership is a deep calling, often
Credited with improving people's mental
Health.

Gregarious by nature, is Homo Sapiens:
The loner, the hermit, is by far the exception
That proves the rule. For companionship we
Slake such a thirst. Even I can see the rewards
That pets supply to their owners, and in a
Way, vicariously I guess, to me.

EURO 24

Many months before the opening
Whistle sounds, this great tournament
Casts its spell – a footballing nation
Seized in great anticipation, awaiting
The fateful Draw, with punditry far
And wide – who will be the anointed
Few, to form the England football side.

For nothing, short of some supernatural
Spell, could so lift the football fraternity
Out of itself, up where plain English
Language will not do. What lies out there,
Almost within our grasp, what celestial
Destiny awaits the Icons, the Legends, the
Stars of our Beautiful Game – but Glory;
Yes, that's the word, Glory – the splendour
Of Heaven Itself.

On the fateful day, the pre-match liturgy,
The 'Build-up' on television lasts almost as
Long as the match will last.

Such a promising preamble, the
Match itself is unlikely to 'match':
Solemn divination of the runes, the
Starting line-up, formations four-three-
Three or four-four-two; state of the pitch,
The danger-men, attack mentality;
Only a stellar performance will do.

Only then, emerging from the tunnel,
Do the stars begin to lose their sheen,
And words must begin to say pretty much
What they mean.
On to the pitch they file, hand-in-hand
Each, with a lucky young child, an uplifting
Sight to see: The greatest day in the life
Of each young child, might have been
Greater still, if the soccer star had 'noticed'
Him or her, shared a friendly word or two,
And smiled.
After the lusty singing of anthems, there
Follows the emptiest, least convincing of
Gestures:

As if to allay simmering mistrust of
Opponents, instead of due respect, one
Team must file past the other, sporting
Handshakes, each with each: Have you
Ever seen such a hand-flapping travesty
Of goodwill?
At the Referee's whistle, the Spell is broken;
A paler, familiar truth descends. With few
Exceptions, the form shown in their Premier
League games, has somehow been lost along
The way. Some inhibition in the mind, something
English in the mind, it seems to me, is where
The truth begins and ends.
  After fifteen minutes or so, I want to rush to

The touchline, where the full-backs are
Passing laterally, to and fro, to and fro, and
Back to the 'keeper. I want to shout out,
"The game has started, chaps – the match is
Under way!"
And when they do venture a forward pass,
As like as not, a half-back will block it straight
Back to them.

So much, in this vein, was served
Before us – so little of 'we dare to win',
So much of 'we dare not lose'.
Several matches passed like this, with
Only brief, saving moments of inspiration.
Contrasting with this dreary negativity, see
The spirit they summon up from somewhere
When someone actually scores – just
Witness that swarming orgy of adoration.

However we reached the Final, I do not
Know, but reach the Final we narrowly did.
Although we showed a little more resolve,
Our English limbs and our English minds
Were second-best, by some way.
The Spanish played with such freedom of
Mind and limb, such skill, such pace and
Self-assurance. The gap in quality was
Wider than our two-to-one defeat suggests.
England were unimpressive, even in the
Weaker side of the Draw.

Just as conspicuously lacking as their
Competitive spirit, it seems to me, was their
Wider awareness of why they were there:
In the form of an amphitheatre, the very
Design of the stadium should signify.
There are tiers of seats, for many thousands
Of spectators, who have travelled from
Far and wide, paying good money to support
Their favourite football side – travelled and
Paid, to witness a thrilling spectacle.
A thrilling spectacle is just what those English
Footballers are paid to provide.

FACULTIES

Faculties provide our clues: We are
Creatures less of Night than of Day,
Our eyes adapted not to darkness, but
To light.

Awaken we then, to the dawn; curl up
In our blanket of Night.

But what if we made synthetic light?
It could make us creatures not only of Day,
But also of artificial Day, though it be Night.

Faculties provide our clues: We are
Creatures less of Night than of Day,
Our ears adapted not to silence, but
To sound.

A night-time silence better slept away,
Soft in our blanket of Night.

But what if we made synthetic sounds
And noises, industrial clamour, well until
The fading of each day's light? It could
Make us creatures less of the clamorous
Day, than of each artificial, extended Day,
Though it be Night.

Faculties provide our clues: We are
Creatures less of isolation than of proximity
And touch, our fingertips adapted not to
Vacancy but to physical touch, of kindred skin.

Vacancy ever kept at bay with familiar, daily
Reassurances of touch.

Then what of the loner, the withdrawn, the
Shy? Why, tactile Arts, or synthetic kindred
Skin – forms for your fingers to sculpt, or mould;
Pets to stroke, horses to groom – artificially
Keeping in touch, thereby.

Faculties provide our clues; We are less
The insensate than creatures of discrimination,
These two samplers of taste and smell.

Nature's gatekeepers and alarmers,
Against the distasteful, and the harmers.

What then, if in our new-found, lofty minds,
We insist on tastes and smells of superior
Kinds? Then might our minds override our
Senses, in what exotic foods we choose to
Swallow, and just what man-made fragrances
We choose to follow.

PARISH CHURCH

Step into the peace and quiet of an
Empty country church, and you can
Never be alone: The silence there, is
Centuries gone by, of parishioners at
Prayer. There is a fellowship in silence
There; palpable, this silence.
Congregations – mere handful sometimes –
Sometimes forty or more – have knelt
And hoped, through peace and war,
Assembled in those polished pews.

You may stand there, in the nave, facing
That way they all have faced, echoing in
Your mind what that silence has to say:
The call of some Tabernacle, some consecrated
Space, some sanctuary and hope, for such
A stranded human race – and there within,
A conduit and guide, a Minister in Holy Orders,
Leading the way to salvation for the soul.
The silence is eloquent, being at once so
Abstract, and so real.

I gaze about me, in an empty country
Church, such a church in which I sang
Solo, once or twice, at Christmas Time.
I guess, in a sense, we all sing solo, in
Our minds. More comforting then, to
Congregate – together to sing our hymns
Of praise.

In an empty church I gaze about me, and
Muse, sensing a fellowship down the ages
In this meeting-place and fold, for human
Hopes. I guess a parish church never can
Be empty.

Just up the road from here, is the church
Of Saint John the Baptist, in Lea – kept tidy
And welcoming to all by churchwarden
Marion Martin, — which, as a place of worship,
Dates back to the 14th century, though one of
Its remarkable artefacts, a huge, iron-bound
Oaken chest, dates back to the century before.
The oldest bell in the tower was cast in 1350,
In Gloucester.

Once, in the early 'thirteen-hundreds', it
Was a simple 'chapel of ease', in the parish
Of Linton, then consecrated as a church
In 1418. An anchoress, named Isabella,
Lived out her years within its walls.

In daylight hours, parish church doors
Are open to all, the simplest expression of
Welcome there could be, as much a faith in
Humanity as a faith in God – one might say
A love of humanity, as of God.

A parish church is akin to a family tree, a
Provenance of memory. It never can be empty.
It depends as much on benefactors, as they
Depend upon the church. Here at Lea, since
The late nineteenth century, a fine devotional
Fresco, dedicated to John the Baptist, adorns
The north wall, the work of one talented
Benefactress, Maude Berry.

Memorials are here too: As well as for
Those who gave their lives in wartime,
There is the remarkable font, or 'stoup',
Itself dating from the 12th century, dedicated
Not only to the Glory of God, but to one
Sarah Decima Bradney, in 1907.

For seven hundred years or so, right here
In this Tabernacle, this consecrated space –
As indeed for even longer, up and down
Old England – local folk have knelt in
Worship, and blessed hope.
The peace and quiet of an empty parish
Church is, I fancy, the peace and quiet of
All those souls at rest. Alone, by no means,
Is anybody, in here.

Much that is affecting there is, from old
Christian England, and the way it survives,
Against considerable odds – a tide of other
Callings, other Gods – leaving its mark on me.
Though I am no Christian, these days, this
I offer, as my personal hymn of praise.

FLY

How long did it take, to make, to
Evolve, a fly — this much lower form
Of life, than I?

I hope you can agree, that a lower
Form of life than I, it must be, for I am
Writing about a fly, a fly not writing
About me.

However long it took, it cannot write,
No more than I can fly: Well, which the
More to be envied, writing or flight?

I'll bet I'd give more to be able to fly,
Than would a fly, to be able to write.

SPORTSMANSHIP

Essentially, sports are diversions
For us all, competitive games to play –
Not games of chance, but those of skill –
Entertainments, diversions, to add some
Lustre to what can become tedious
Lives. And since 'competition' implies
A winner, a winner implying a loser
Too, it is potentially a drama, a spectacle
For onlookers: That some sports draw
Such a following, surely proves that
They do feed some deep, abiding human
Need.

So we must hope that, wherever lies this
Human need, this thirst, it is for the best
Of motivations, not the worst – that sport
Becomes a civilising adaptation of early,
Primitive man, and not primitive man himself.
What I have in mind is 'sportsmanship', and
How we must distinguish this from the
Necessary skills of the sport.
You may be the most successful
Exponent of your sport, but if 'sport'
Does not embrace a sense of fairness,
Humour and goodwill – a contest purely
Of fitness and of skill – then sport is
A barren diversion indeed.

A true sportsman, on whichever court
Or field of play, shows his opponent all
Due courtesy, and always respects the
Judgements of umpire or referee. He
Does not throw tantrums at a losing game,
Nor roar like King Kong, at a winner.
He never disfigures a football match with
Wilful, egregious fouling.

We have become so used to our sporting 'Stars'
Being crowned and canonised by incontinent
Gushing of language, irrespective of their conduct.
Let us reserve our sober and genuine words of
Praise for those sportsmen and sportswomen
Who illuminate their court or their field of play,
Win or lose, by their demeanour, sporting manners, And
good grace.

LIBERTI

Within such contradictions must all
Societies pave their way – that only
Bound by Rules and Laws, can you and
I find Freedom, to work and worship,
And have our say – the liberty of the
Individual, by public interest circumscribed.
And so there are 'boundaries' aplenty,
'Barriers' and 'glass ceilings', for the
Restless, the indignant and the hard-done-by
To challenge, or defy, sometimes with
Such good cause.

In less legalistic matters too, in customs and
Conventions, something similar moves us –
All the way from common sense to vanity,
And pettiness. Among the more sensible
Loosening of old conventions was a freedom
In applause: In my early days, even the way
Of cheering was prescribed.

'Three cheers', it had to be, a leader
Shouting "Hip-Hip" then a chorus of
"Hooray" or "Hurrah" – thrice over.
Often then, a lusty rendering of "For he's
A jolly good fellow..."
The modern way is spontaneous yelping
And 'whooping', a liberated barrage of cheers.

On a less dramatic scale, back in the Sixties
Or Seventies, a trend among free-thinkers
Was to abandon Capital letters for beginning
People's names, and even for starting a sentence.
Lower-case letters throughout, were an
Emphatic blow struck for freedom – from
Petty micro-repression, as modern folk might say.

Short-lived as this all was, an allied trend,
Relating to words, is lasting so much longer.
It falls somewhere between the age-old way
Of pet-naming from formal names, and a touch
Of vanity in having a name few other people have.

About a generation ago, it germinated:
Some lady, somewhere, let me call her
Judith, was befriended as Judy, and decided
That the terminal 'y' was too common by
Far. She changed it to 'i' – this terminal 'i'
Not to be the ending 'i' of Rabbi, but that of
Kiwi – to sound like the original 'y', indeed.

How disappointed she must have been, when
Along came Salli and Jenni, Jacki, Suzi, Mari,
Rosi, Toni and Cheri – making commonplace
What was intended to be exclusive.

It would be silli of me to mock human vaniti,
For I am part of it. Something endearing there
Is, about our fallibiliti; plenty of good humour,
And much ironi are to be found, in our natural
Thirst for Liberti.

FEATHER

I contemplate you too, as common as
A blade of grass, as any leaf upon a
Tree; you too, in your feathering filigree,
Never cease to tease my mind to
Understand quite what here before me,
In amazement, I do see.
My imagination you so tease, through
Aeons, incremental aeons – how from
Base Reptilia so risen, so exalted, are
The Birds – adaptations minuscule per
Million year, refining for purpose each
Million year, towards your present
Kinship with our skies.
If all of this, from aeons past, what, for
Goodness sake, from aeons yet to come?
The same might be posed, of our Human
Kind, but with an added phenomenon,
This human mind: Your progress from the
Forest floor up to our skies, would pass
Unknown, unrecognised, were there no
Human mind, no imagination so to tease.
That individual bird, among countless
Thousands, from whose wing you were
Lost, or plucked, no more knew of me,
Than I of that passing bird. Birds may
Never know what compliments we pay
When we deck our head-dress with feathers,

Our flags and badges and banners with
Proud feathers – as if there is something of
Birds which we so envy, and so covet: For
All its power, its range, its height, Aviation
Merely masquerades as Flight.

But what, for Goodness sake, from aeons more?
As every beautician knows, every camera,
Every ego, every mirror knows, and every
Work of Art implies, in vanity and preening
Are what we people specialise. It will hardly
Take us by surprise, when each and every follicle,
Every single human hair, into a splendid feather
Will evolve, nay, radiate, and upon such iridescent,
Ostentatious, angelic, feathering Wings, shall we Human
Beings soar, rightfully enthroned, exalted, Sovereign of our
Skies.

SALVATION

By way of confirming Christ's authority
As the Son of God, the Miracles are, by
Definition, phenomena supernatural.
Browsing through them, I read that they
Are 'documented by eyewitnesses and
Recorded in biblical history'.
Mostly they are healings, but there is
Walking on water, turning water into wine,
And several raisings from the dead,
Including the Resurrection itself.
They are said to serve a 'specific purpose
In God's plan of Salvation for humankind'.
This notion of Salvation it is, which draws
Me here; something like Salvation is
Devoutly to be wished.

For that which is separable from our mortal
Remains, and persists beyond the grave,
Salvation is Heavenly deliverance from
Eternal damnation.

This, I do not mock, though I see through
Different eyes – assuming that death is death,
Absolute, unqualified.

If we believe that, far from being divinely
Appointed, we are no more divine than our
Kindred apes; that in a chance divergence
We swung away from the family tree, with
Strange new faculties, perplexities of the brain,
It is Salvation of our own that we must seek.
Lost souls all, we must locate ourselves in
This empty vastness, take a compass bearing,
As it were, on some kind of lighthouse, be it
A Father God or a Mother Earth – divinity
Or natural history.
Down here on Earth, we have our 'Miracles'
Too, phenomena of the natural kind –
Selective adaptations, the insect and the flower,
The germination of a seed, the division of cells
And metamorphoses; the coding of inheritance
In DNA – pretty well scrutinised all, in
Our human science. This being a matter of
Heart and soul, though I must take the earthly
Way, Salvation blessed either way.

IMROPRIETY

On this opening night, we must look our
Best. Rehearsals over, members of the
Orchestra in their formal evening wear,
Respectfully, are dressed. Without exception
The audience too is dressed for the occasion.
By such courtesies are such events enhanced.

So, stepping on to the conductor's podium,
And reaching for my baton, I falter, aware
Of impropriety – for what may be seen to
Traduce the memories of both tonight's composers.
With what sensitivity can I interpret each score,
When I feel the audience staring at me? How to
Inspire with looks and gestures so self-consciously?
How can I live in the thrill of the music, bring out
Inflections and tempo, articulate poignant phrases,
Sense when to bring in the flutes and bassoons?
When the success of the evening, upon me
Principally rides, whatever possessed me, this
Afternoon, to go out and have – madness, I know –
A 'short-back-and-sides'?

DUVET

It sounds decidedly posh and French,
You know, so you have to say it in the
Francophile way – not like 'you bet', but
Like 'hooray' — but oh, give me sheets and
Blankets any day.
For reclining horizontally, and thus to sleep,
Is the overriding purpose of a bed, with
Covers to keep you cosy for the night –
Upon and under sheets, smoothing and
Cooling to the touch, with one or two or
Three or four blankets, that tuck in down
The sides, according to your needs.
It is a provision handed down through
Centuries past, that you may regulate your
Bedding, by peeling back a blanket or two,
As you require, for a deep and dreamless sleep.
Then along came science, and progress,
And those French, to pay us back for Agincourt
And Waterloo: They seem to have a grudge
Against me.

Wherever I book in somewhere these
Days, summertime or wintertime, I can
Be sure of some gross, smothering duvet,
Tog-rated for the Northern Pole, an all-or-nothing
Wretched duvet: There is no sleep under
Here, but to gasp and sweat until half-past
Two, when I kick the bleeder off, and freeze
Until the dawn. Oh, give me sheets and
Blankets any day. Am I supposed to bring
My own? It's not just bed and breakfast
I pay for; it's breakfast after a damn good sleep.

It's all a conspiracy, I'm sure, to render
British people sleepless and irritable, reduce
The nation to chronic peevishness, ripe for
Surrender to foreign annexation.

I bet they don't have duvets in Heaven.
I'm not going, if they do: Eternity under
A duvet? My idea of … you know damn well.

DADDY-LONG-LEGS

Such an event happens, I imagine, a million
Times every day, unremarked, unnoticed,
Without any thought to attach to it; it is
Better off, I guess, without a thought.
From its sudden start, I was witness: All in
That instant, I opened the door to the porch,
That crane-fly got stuck, and that small spider
Struck.
However many million years it took spiders
To evolve, and to spin sticky threads, the
Process must have adapted itself to that of
Insects like the crane-fly – or else there is a
Department in Spider Heaven, tasked with
Designing insects with long, dangling legs —
For entanglement, Heaven-sent.

The first few minutes were a frenzied thrashing
About of the hapless fly, wings quivering
Desperately, but legs entwined, and the spider
Clinging, to inject its venom.

Several tense minutes of writhing and twisting
Led only to more entanglement. However the
Crane-fly thrashed about, the outcome never
Was in doubt. Before long, the insect was still –
Probably not dead, but numbed by the spider's
Venom. A few minutes later, the predator hauled
Its prey, utterly immobilised, into its dark corner,
A couple of weeks' rations, I imagine.
There was nothing new or surprising about it, but
What a transfixing few minutes to witness it.

I might as well admire the brilliance of that spider,
Its ingenuity, swiftness, deadly efficiency – and yet
My overriding sentiment was a sympathy for that
Fly – and I'm left to wonder why.
I might as well, with a rod and line, haul out a trout,
Thrashing frantically, from a stream, kill it, and enjoy
It for my supper, without it troubling my mind too
Much. And yet I felt sympathy for that fly, and I
Wonder why.
The following morning, in the porch, I saw another
Crane-fly. I put it outside, to save its life, and I'm
Left to wonder why.

FJORD

Rocks and seas, or images of these,
And possibilities, do contend within
Us; stubbornness beset by impatience.
Both a rock and a sea, aspects of you
And me so elementary that some Fjord
State of mind must be within our reach.

Once the seas have claimed all they are
Able to claim, and the rocks have yielded
All they have to yield, what remains is
That serene stillness of the Fjord, that
Apparent sense of differences resolved:
A state of grace.

The way towards those Fjord waters,
Towards that calmer place, Humility,
Unerringly, will show us. In the service
Less of ourselves and more of others,
Those quieter inlets may we find, along
Some peaceful Fjord of the mind.

HYPOTHESIS

Our cabin in the cruise ship was one
Of those around the promenade deck,
Where passengers could stroll, or stride
Out briskly, doing 'circuits' to keep fit,
Whether in harbour or at sea.
Our fears of having no privacy, open to
Inspection by every passer-by, were soon
Allayed; one-way glass. We could observe,
Without being observed.

People-watching, at our leisure, day by day,
Soon revealed an unexpected trend: Almost
Every promenader opted for an anticlockwise
Circuit: Counter-clockwise, as viewed from
Above – from forward to aft down the port
Side, around the stern, and back forward, up
The starboard side. Quite astonishing, day
After day, the predominance of this; not one
Hundred per cent, but not far short: Only an
Occasional couple, or individual, chose
Clockwise, against the flow.

Some natural reason for this, there must be
Though, come to think of it, little to do with
Being at sea.
To some such natural priming must we be
In thrall, or why this cultural curvature of
Ours, at all?
Or why, invariably, the laps of our athletics
Tracks, the steeplechasers' course, the Formula
One circuit, all of left-hand bends?
Why the skaters at the rink, the dancers at the
Ball, the fairground carousel, anticlockwise all?
Of such natural 'priming', it seems we are
Endowed, inwardly formed for wheeling left,
Straightening out, then wheeling left again.

It could be a matter, I guess, of 'handedness'.
We right-handers outnumber the lefties by more
Than ten-to-one – just about that disparity around
The promenade deck, where a handful, dare I say,
Who chose the clockwise way, may well have been
Helpless lefties, anticipating right-hand bends.

SWEETBREADS

"You wouldn't eat those, Chollie, if you
Knew what they were," said Dave, as the
Pair sitting with him, opposite me, chuckled
Knowingly. I had selected 'sweetbreads',
When the steward came with the menu.

Many years ago, that was, but I still recall
My embarrassment, my sense of ignorance.
It was easy to guess, from their amusement,
What part of the animal those 'sweetbreads'
Must have been.

Later, consulting my dictionary, I found
That 'sweetbreads' were sometimes the thymus
Gland, sometimes the pancreas, of the animal,
Used for food. I had not known this, but nor
Had those other fellows, I'd say, for neither
Of those organs would likely have evoked
Their knowing chuckles.

There is a quiet satisfaction, on recall,
With a somewhat perverse and personal
Shine, for the ignorance was theirs, as
Well as mine.

It is too long since, to know what those
Sweetbreads tasted like, but if they had
Been what those fellows had in mind, and
If those tasty morsels slipped down very well –
Then what the hell?

REVELATION

Were it possible to unpick the interlocking
Threads with which my life is patterned,
Is bound, and as it were, my lifeclock wound,
The most prominent strand would be the
Status, in this country, of the female, vis-à-vis
The male.

It was a simpler, backward-looking world —
That for which I was prepared, enrolled –
In which menfolk did the telling; womenfolk,
What they were told.

Manifest and undisputed, was that Pecking-
Order in our home: Hanging on hooks, behind
Our kitchen door, were two towels, one for our
Father, the other for his wife and three children.
That was Dad's chair; that, Dad's end of the
Settee; that was Dad's shelf, where he kept
His watch, his nail-scissors, his fountain-pen,
His pipe and tobacco.

An inflexible man, of few words and limited
Awareness, he ruled with a brooding silence,
And such an implied toughness, that even
Without the appeasing mildness of our mother,
He was to prevail. That he would carelessly
Break wind, and then say 'crash', showed just
How men were entitled to be – coarse and
Brash, unrestrained by finer feelings.

Of a Friday evening, go to the local 'picture-house'
And what would I see? Back in the 'Forties',
Those Cowboy films were machismo writ large:
Any woman in the story shielded her tender
Eyes while saloon disputes were settled by
Crashing chairs and flailing masculine fists.
If it was a Tarzan film, Johnny Weissmuller
Would put it succinctly – "Tarzan go now;
Jane stay". Tarzan went, of course; Jane stayed.

An unwelcoming world I found, therefore, when
I left home.

Sure, the girls wore tiny watches, carried
Impractical pretty hankies, walked arm-in-
Arm for security. Sure, they lingered over
'Babycham' or half a shandy in the Lounge
Bar, while the lads drank pints – but they
Had minds of their own, and will-power
Of their own, these girls. This world out here
Was no place for 'Tarzans', who often were
Outshone by their 'Janes'.
Far from being helpless, over-emotional
Creatures, they clearly had some understanding,
Some stability, of a kind unknown to us males.
Less to be directed, than consulted, it seemed,
Were females.

Irony and paradox everywhere; a sad 'Pathetic
Fallacy' was in the air, through which came
Filtering, a general Truth – that greater height
And weight, and physical strength were, in our
Modern world, diminishing credentials.

The challenge to manliness was to recognise just
Who was dependent upon whom – to see that
Much of our clowning and swagger arose from
Weaknesses.
Patronising of the female was very likely our
Discomfort, in disguise – and what a limited man
I must have appeared, through female eyes.

CRIMINAL

Many and debatable, I accept, are
Criminality's causes, but so few crimes
Are committed without a degree of
Personal choice, from the opportunist
Theft, to the elaborate and merciless 'scam'.

Put another way, aside from a chronically
Amoral few, most criminals know that
What they do is antisocial, and often ruthless,
But the chance of personal gain simply
Overrides any innocent victim's pain.
Suppose, into the darkness of the criminal
Mind, we were to crawl, holding before us
A lamp of curiosity – what ever might we find?
Somehow, somewhere, within this ancient
Labyrinth, all our abstract nouns were spawned,
And grew, and here forever, delineate a Mind.
This being a criminal mind, even in this maze
Of cells and chambers, the lodgings of our
Abstract nouns denote themselves as we might infer –
Commodious for perversities, hovels for the virtues.

On this landing up here, above those spiral steps,
In place of enlightenment, there is dusk. The
Honeycomb of social cells, hermit spaces now —
Here are Kindness, Honour, unoccupied; over
There Integrity, deserted – Empathy, Conscience,
Barren spaces now.

It is a dark descent from here, down those spiral
Steps, with a stink of moral putrefaction in the air.
Down through the tunnels of Pride and Greed, past
Those anterooms of Ego, down to the flashiest
Chamber of all, where the soul of the man himself
May squat, to preen himself, admire himself, idle
And gloat, and feed, flicking crumbs to the mind-rats
Squabbling around his feet for some of his scraps.
So aptly named as Arrogance, this chamber, where
He fattens his days, rehearsing future deceptions,
Grinning at the wailings of those he has fooled,
And impoverished. Blithely unaware that he is as
Welcome in society as an aching belly, he squats
Amongst his profits in his Basement Chamber,
Hung with portraits of himself and, no doubt,
Of Machiavelli.

No less, I'd say, than we expected to find,
Within the depths of a criminal mind.

And if this fellow, one day, should fall
Upon hard times, and turn for help to our
Welfare State, can you imagine a more
Challenging call upon our Humanity,
Than finding this criminal at our Mercy?

FLORA

Inseparably, has our story unfolded,
As Fauna, from our Flora. Nothing more
Consequential then, that we should so
Borrow from those plants, to express
Beginnings and developments of all
Manner of things as 'seeded', 'rooted',
'Stemmed' and 'flowered'. Deep-rooted
Are flowers, in our folklore.
How they appealed to imagination, in
Names like Foxglove, Ladies' Fingers,
Shepherd's Purse, Goat's Beard.
How we borrowed back some names to
Name ourselves, as Violet, Daisy and Lily,
And how we endow them with our own
Sentiments, as Bluebell for Constancy,
Cyclamen for Diffidence, Snowdrop for Hope.
Just as a person's height, can lend a certain
Presence, so with a blossom on its lofty stem,
Promoted, elevated, to be noticed – bright dress
And fragrance her stock-in-trade – Nature's
Temptress after all.
The fragility, it may be, of a flower, that
Lends it such compelling power: We must
Not touch those petals, but feel what they
Have to say. They form a beauty at its best,
No finger-touch can better: A fragility, I say,
No sooner to flourish, than to wither away.

And in this flourishing, this serving of its
Purpose, then withering away, there surely
Is a kindred eloquence, in flowers, for what
You and I are often at a loss to say.

No shock, no bereavement, joy nor celebration,
Can we quite articulate, without flowers in
Their pomp and pride – from that lonely wreath
At the roadside, where some poor soul has died,
To the 'buttonhole' at a wedding, and a bouquet
For the bride; from the poppy on Remembrance
Day, to poignancy in flowers upon a coffin.

They so embellish human feelings – their
Fragility, I feel sure, lending form and colour
To whatever we might wish to say.

"DOUG"

The customary playing of that song
'My Way', at the closing stage of a funeral,
Was never more fitting than at the passing
Of old Doug Allen. If ever there lived
A man who had ploughed his own furrow,
It was he.
As his new next-door neighbour, I heard him
Clearly, before I met him. His was the voice
Heard, across the gardens. Self-confidence
Personified, was Douglas, as of a man
Conscious of a mission in life – never idle,
Constructing things, repairing things, holding
Forth with such authority on many topics,
Whether fully understood, or not.

As sociable as anyone could wish, was Douglas;
Neighbourliness second nature to him.
I personally was indebted to him for help,
When I was in need. Thus, he had numerous
Friends and passing acquaintances, sociability
And enthusiasm, his twin strengths.

Nor was there a more loyal Englishman:
Permanently, from a pole in their garden,
Flies the Union Flag, and I would wish it to
Do so evermore, as a tribute to Douglas,
And all of his kind. In his home are
Artefacts of times gone by, an antique
Dialling telephone, an ornate early cash
Till. In our age of personal mobile phones,

Those red public phone-boxes are being
Removed from the streets. Two of them
Are safe in his garden now, 'rescued' by
Douglas; some essence of Old England
Preserved.
In Paula, he could not have had a more
Dependable wife. In their marriage of
Nigh-on sixty years, she bore him three sons,
And supported all his enterprises, such as
His travels to vintage vehicle rallies.
From Paula it was, that I learned of Doug's
Earlier work on the parish council, including
His successful efforts to keep open Lea
School, when it was facing closure.

This man, who had raised much money for
Charities, had been a 'force for good'.
As an extrovert, he lived on the surface,
As it were: What you saw was what you got.
"Doug was an open case", was the way
Paula put it. His bark was worse than his bite;
Ill-tempered moments soon over and done with.

"It's quieter here now", said Paula, with a smile.
Without Doug, it is emptier, too.

EXPECTATION

Perhaps, my love, we need to dwell a pause,
Both for my sake and for yours,
On what is wise and what is best,
Before this wave of expectation crests.

Have we been hearing, without listening?
Have we been looking, without seeing?
Have we been dreaming, but never thinking
Of what is wise, and what is best?

Are we smiling merely with our lips,
Touching, barely, with our fingertips –
Touching, but yet hardly feeling
For what is wise, what is best?

So seductive it is, to fall
For Old Nature's siren call.
But humans are bound by other strings –
Boring, sensible, practical things.

Yet if, my love, after sensible pause,
Both for my sake, and for yours –
We do listen, and find, we're leaving
Any doubts behind – as two lovers
Of a single mind, passing this cautious,
Sensible test, of what is wise and
What is best –

Then let this wave of expectation burst,
And slake we, of this natural thirst.

WATERFALL

Waters will fall, just as, unsupported,
Must we all, for there is a yielding that
We share, a vulnerability we share, to
Forces elemental.
From the earliest leaching and seeping
Through those craggy mountain flanks,
Springs and trickles must but weave
The least resistant way, motivated, we
May say, by some eternal ocean out
There, of which they seem aware.

Here and there, they will appear to pause,
And paddle, in tributary pools, but their
Fall has been so scoured and slicked, as
Never to be avoided.
And so, waters will fall, and what easier
Way than over an edge – free fall – an
Unsupported yielding, as if in trust or
Hope, a leap of faith, a waterfall, finding
Some presence there, as if suspended in
The air, which you and I may sense, and share.

Here is affirmation of a kind, to mesmerise
A human mind. Shaking out its feathery
Tresses, the water falls yet falling, appears
To stay right there: The water? It falls; the
Waterfall stays, teasing and compelling our
Human gaze.

We do not watch a river go by. The water
Passes; the river stays. While we hark to
The waterfall's hushing, delight in rainbow
Scatterings of sunlight in its mist and haze,
May it be some constancy in our shifting
World, that so captivates our human gaze?

CONGRATULATIONS

Congratulations, Mister Carey. Your new
Appointment is the least that you deserve.
Every school where you have taught, toiling
At the 'chalkface', supplied to us the same
Report — pupils of yours so motivated,
Incentivised and energised. Classroom
Teachers of such calibre, such popularity,
So difficult to find.
In appointing you as Head of School, the
Governors on the Board relieve you now of
All that classroom teaching – 'timetable-free'
You shall be – and hope that your new status,
And salary, will be compensation, and reward.

Self-respecting vocations everywhere, are bound
To find enlightenment there. Where would our
Country be, without professional teachers to
Inspire, to teach? If our country cannot grow
From it, benefit and enrich itself from it, what
Is the purpose of education?

Congratulations, Doctor Fletcher. So richly
Deserved is your new promotion. Reports
From colleagues and patients over the years,
Point clearly to this professional elevation.
We hope you will understand that the status
Of Consultant, despite its name, confines you
To administrative duties, exempting you
From any further treatment of patients.

Congratulations, Reverend Brewer. Your
Commitment in the Faith, your holiness,
Have never been in doubt. After twenty
Years in holy orders, this Bishopric is your
Reward. You will understand that your
New status relieves and exempts you from
Any further preaching, or conducting of
Religious services.

Congratulations, Mister Grainger. We have
So many impressive, glowing reports, before,
During and since your Pupillage.
Here is your reward: On being appointed
As Barrister, you now are freed, evermore,
From the tedious 'hassle' of acting as Counsel,
In Court.

If there is anything sillier, less responsible,
Less forgivable, less cost-effective, than a
Counsel who may not counsel, a Consultant
You may not consult, or a Preacher who
May not preach, it surely is a Teacher – yes,
A Teacher — who does not teach.

ENGLISH

Unlike our previous, traditional, Head of
English, the new man was of a different
Mould: New ways of teaching the subject,
Obviously better than the old.
In the jargon of the day, the new man had
A 'laid-back', 'freed-up' stance; the potential
Of poems and novels and plays to influence
Minds was all. The language itself, in its
Precision, its nuances, its grammar, all but
A tiresome, stuffy irrelevance. Never mind
The medium; the message was all. Even in
Verse, bound closest to its language, poetry
Well second best, to the sentiments expressed.
That Literature's power to influence, rides
So much on rhetorical skills in the writer,
Through sentence structure, punctuation,
Imagery, irony, allusion, idiom, felicitous
Choice of words, and so on, did not seem to
Concern our new man, so much so that
I wondered if the Department, of which he
Was Head, deserved a more accurate name.

A humanitarian purpose, this subject in
Schools always has served, but to neglect
The medium itself, would seem to invite
A more accurate label than 'English' –
Head of Enlightenment, perhaps; Equality,
Discrimination, Colonial Penance, Liberation.

A pleasant and courteous fellow, was our
New man, but his subject matter seldom
Was 'English'. That the cuttings he kept,
For use in class, were all from the Guardian,
Or the Observer, seemed consistent with
His concern about the layout of classrooms.
Desks in rows were too formal for him, too
Regimented, I suppose, with all eyes on the
Teacher. He would have clusters of desks,
With circles of pupils, several with their
Backs to him. We were to be progressive,
'Freed-up', 'laid-back'.

If this is to be our way ahead, then let us
Simply label his subject as Book Reading,
And let us be sure to provide, in the earlier
School years, a dedicated appreciation of
English Grammar, which will shed much
Light on those poems, novels and plays.

One of the finest flowerings of Humanity,
Is this language of ours. Nothing better
Equips and empowers us, to deal with any
Study, or any circumstance we may face
In life, than the richness of this language
We have inherited from our forbears,
Down the centuries.

WHEREWITHAL

What one receives, and where one Banks,
Serve both, as clues to where one ranks.
Emoluments, or Pay.
What one earns, one does not say, but
Which will point promotion's way,
Emoluments, or Pay.
Earn by months, never by weeks,
If eminence is what one seeks.
Emoluments, or Pay.
One's units of prestige are found
In euphemisms to the pound.
Emoluments, or Pay.

Remuneration, Salary, Wages –
One never mentions Money.

In taking Holy Orders, one must say,
Our clergyfolk have found one way
Of keeping vulgar cash at bay –
The sanctity of Stipends, any day.

BODY LANGUAGE

Much raising of eyebrows was there, much
Rolling of eyes, not to say wrinkling of noses,
Among her friends, when it was clear that
He was smiling upon her.
Such a wagging of tongues was there, such
Nodding, head-shaking and frankly, such
Scratching of heads too, when he smiled
Upon her.

For was he not the most stoney-faced and
Tight-lipped of fellows, with that stiff-upper-lip
Manner, and that affectedly furrowed brow?
And was he not toe-curlingly arrogant? Did he
Not sniffily thumb his nose at common folk,
And was he not so shiveringly honey-tongued?

And how the flesh did creep, and the jaws did
Sag, at his oily, finger-licking blandishments.
It was when she blushingly fluttered her eyelids
At him, that they could stomach it no more.

Friends no more, they gave her the cold
Shoulder, turning their backs on her. How
Her ears would burn, if she could hear them.

How gut-wrenching for her now, to see his
Mean face lighting up, at her discomfiture.
Such a hair-raising, knee-jerk reaction was
There! With blazing eyes and curling lips,
She vented her spleen, and told him explicitly
Where to go.

And then, what a heart-stopping was there,
Such watering of eyes was there, amongst
Her friends-once-more – enough to bring a
Lump to the throat, and a tingle to the spine.

ALCHEMY

In all this natural world around us, an
Evolutionary tale is told, of incremental
Changes, ages long – while Homo Sapiens
Has a 'History', instead, as if we don't
Belong.
All other creatures than we, it would
Appear, have turned out to be what they
Were best-suited to be. How much more
Formed for the sea, can the shark or the
Barnacle be? All other species too, just
As a fait accompli. Attributes too, best-
Suited and honed – the predator's stealth,
The alertness of prey, the patience of spiders.

Hominid, hunter-gatherers, early man:
Humanity is ours, History is ours, as if
We were starting over again, and with
Such an awareness of ourselves, existing,
In the passing of time.

Though of the commonest matter made,
For better or for worse, blessing or curse,
Some wondrous 'Alchemy' has broached
Our brain, allowing forth imagination,
And all the rest.
We are moved to speak of an Underworld,
As if it were deep beneath us, and of a
Heaven, so far above us yet both, we may
Be sure, reside within us, offspring of our
Own, by this strange 'Alchemy', so begotten.

Allowing forth, I say, powers of ours, though
Many wonderful and wise, many others
Otherwise – rather like a Disobedience in
The Garden: An Original Sin. While Nature
Forms and shapes the world, in her own
Sweet time, mankind seems impatient to
Adapt our parent world, to his own shallow
Fancies, at great environmental cost.

How believable it was, back then – this
'Alchemy' turning base metal into gold,
I cannot say.

Believable, is History, but I'd like to think
It has a shaping, a forming, and a process to
Refine, leading to what we are best-suited
To be – and may that consummation be
A state of Earthly Grace, Homo Sapiens Benign.

And let our human story so be told, of Alchemy
Turning human baseness into human gold.

THE UNDERSIGNED

A most confident and popular 'Madam
Chairman' of our Club was she, contentedly
Over-weight, with an easy, cultured air
About her, evidently happy at home.

Married well, one felt, had she; as clearly
Married well had he.

One thing that parked her in my mind, so
That I recall it even now, was her somewhat
Coy way of confiding in me her pride in
Her husband.

A man I'd never met, he held a senior post in
Some public sector Department, charged with
Making crucial recommendations to government.

Her tribute was no less sincere for being oblique
And implied:
"His is the last signature to go on the Paper".

REFERENDA

Dear Government, it would be, I promise
You, consistent with Democracy, now and
Again to consult the people, on matters of
National concern – not only at Election Time
But in-between times as well – the occasional
Referendum, not binding of course, but
Worth knowing of the national mood.

Suitable questions, not vague but precise,
Might be posed, on Education, Health care,
Foreign policy, Defence, Lords reform, and
So on – to sound out what might be construed,
In quite literal terms, as common sense.
Ask us.
That you do not ask us, may tell us that you
Neither care, nor wish to know.

How satisfying it would be, dear Government,
To feel you acting on our behalf, in our best
Interests, tackling domestic affairs –

Affairs like freedom of speech, crime and
Punishment, proportional representation,
Foreign ownership of our Companies,
'Dumbing down' of language and standards
Of broadcasting, and overdue reforms of
The law.
Ask us.

On so many topics, it seems to me, policies
Run counter to what the people would
Have them be, and some, notably immigration,
Run counter to common observation, and
To human nature as well. Yes, dear Government,
Immigration: Along with neglect of our Armed
Forces, this is the chief concern for me.
If only you had asked me.
Humanitarian asylum for genuine refugees is
One thing, open borders quite another.
Overcrowding, faster than we can build houses,
Overloading of public services; split communities;
Inter-cultural tensions.

It was all so foreseeable, 'way back when';
Warnings were sounded, way back then.
We were heading for trouble.

Dear Government, if only you had asked us,
Held a Referendum,
We could have warned you.
I could have warned you.
I could have told you so,
Fifty frolicking years ago.

CIGARETTES

A few memories of smoking re-visit me
Now. Furtively, around age fifteen, I tried
My first few cigarettes. The peak period of
Smoking, in this country, it must have been,
Well before the link was made, with cancer,
A rite of passage to adulthood, I suppose,
And a mainly masculine thing to do.

Ritual indeed, around 'cigs', or 'fags', 'tailor-
Made' or roll-your-own: Cigarette cases,
Lighters, lighter fuel. Never mind the smoker's
Cough, smelly ash-trays, nicotine fingers –
Smoking was promoted as calming for the
Nerves, an aid to concentration, a friend
In your loneliness, and what's more, at the
Cinema, rugged Hollywood heroes were
Consummate smokers.
Ritual indeed, in company, offering them
Around, knowingly comparing brands; they
Went well, with a few drinks.

Back then, our trains had not the open-plan
Carriages of today, but small compartments
Linked by a side corridor. There were first,
Second and even third-class carriages, clearly
Marked as Smoking or Non-Smoking. Two
Separate moments are imprinted on my mind.

In the first, preening myself I suppose, as a
Budding young fellow with grown-up manners,
I asked if anyone would mind if I smoked.
Permission was granted, in a way that left me
Smarting, in my corner, "You can burst into
Flames, for all I care".

In the second, two or three of us were smoking
In a 'Non-Smoker', when the Guard came and
Sternly rebuked us. After he'd gone, one fellow
Unforgettably declared, "Us orta told'n us
Coont read, dinnus"!

What followed, of course, this posturing
Stage, was a dependence, not far short of
Addiction, on smoking, and this meant
Wasting a good deal of money on the habit –
An expensive way to damage your health.
It was a few years before the silliness of
It came to me, but at the start, I guess it did
Have some soothing effect, on a somewhat
Nervous young lad.

It is many years since I quit the tobacco habit,
And so in the long run my health has not
Suffered. I'm sure the fashionable ritual of it
All did lend a certain 'street-cred' or kudos
To that boy who so lacked personality and
Self-esteem.

MISCAST

Time was, when Prime Ministers were
Seldom seen nor heard, as they directed
The nation's affairs – only written about
For the very few, in those illiterate days.
Impersonal, aloof, aloft, they were but
Names. How different now, out in the
Light, before world cameras; exposure,
Scrutiny, before a less deferential public
And press. Yet what hope have we now,
Of perceiving wisdom, or judgement,
Through a fog of oratory, personality,
Charisma?
"She came out second best", in the televised
'Head-to-head', was what the papers said, and
"Fancy, choosing that dress to wear" – clearly
Throwing doubt on how she might acquit
Herself at meetings of foreign Leaders.
How vague she seemed, at the televised 'press
Conference', under hostile fire from journalists –
Clearly casting doubt on how she might direct
Her Cabinet, forming coherent policies, in office.

On that Sunday morning televised interview,
Watched by millions, how awkward and self-
Conscious she appeared, illustrating clearly
What a misfit she would be, upon the world's
Political stage.

And her unpolished guilelessness at the weekly
Panto, PMQ's – how reassuring was this, and
What might be inferred, of her mastery of her
Brief, her loyalty to the Crown, her understanding
Of the British people, her talent for negotiation –
How indicative might this be, of anything at all?

Not a whit, we may be sure, for utterly superficial
Is all this – mere performance, theatre, prostituting
Politics to show-business, and the stage.

In a functioning Democracy, let our politicians,
Our Prime Ministers, be our representatives, our
Members of Parliament, not 'Members of the Cast',
As Dramatis Personae.

CHRISTMAS

Long, long, before it was so named, our
Winter solstice must have been awaited,
Anticipated, in the shortening days – the
Young, comforted by the old – for a great
Mystery is foretold: The light will surely
Come again. They say it always does so.

Believe, you must, and take it on trust, we
Are not forgotten: That which will provide,
Is surely on our human side.
No sooner past the solstice, at Christmastide,
The Pagan and the Christian, side by side.

More than birth, a rebirth is this, Darkness into
Light, everlasting providence, demonstrable –
The Christian and the Pagan, sharing space and
Meaning.

How tempting to say, that in a way, in welcoming
The Christmas Child, are God and Nature reconciled.

VILLAGE STORES

From earlier days our footpaths, our trails,
Would follow the natural lie of the land, and
Where our trails would cross, there, by and
By, an ancient parish church would stand;
As likely, an Inn be found, a travellers'
Meeting-place and rest.
Just so here, where trails intersect, watered
By natural streams, what else would make
This meeting-place a Village, but a local shop?
An ancient parish church we have; a medieval
Inn we have, and now, to complete the people's
Needs, serving us all, the Lea Village Stores.

For, further to its core purpose of selling and
Buying, come benefits incidental, less tangible,
A social space keeping people in touch, a daily
Passing of pleasantries, the odd exchange of
Gossip, a sense of community, a focal point
Apart from the church, and the Inn – continuity,
Stability — and invariably, a sense of welcome.

It would soon be felt by customers, if the
Welcome were simply a 'Business' one.
But not here. The welcome of Mark and
Michelle is genuine, and warm.
As impressive as the sheer range of items
For sale – as newsagents, grocers, licensed
General stores – they are purveyors also
Of goodwill. All strangers are welcome;
Village customers almost as friends, known
By name. Good nature personified, indeed.
Long hours, seven days a week, year-round
Their Stores are open. They make deliveries too.

The only flaw that I can see, if flaw it be, is
Mark's suspicious tendency: When I ask for
A 'Newcastle' or two, for my mate, he seems
To suspect they are really for me.
The very idea.

FISH KNIFE

In our cruise-ship restaurant, when we
Had ordered from the dinner menu, the
Waiter would return to the table and, for
Those who had ordered fish, replace each
Conventional knife with this forbidding
Instrument.
Not fork, nor spoon, and masquerading
As a knife, this diminutive harpoon, for
Discriminating diners, makes me wonder
At the nature of its task, that motivated its
Designers.
This was no razor-sharp fish-knife at the
Factory, for filleting or skinning, nor merely
That fancy slice hammered thin and flat in
A vaguely piscine shape, to amuse the finer
Diners.
This was conceived on another plane, on
Several planes indeed, angled and angled
Again, in three dimensions, so specialised
That the unenlightened diner is left to ponder
The nature of its task, and whence the inspiration.

Based on a Bricky's mortar trowel perhaps,
Or an ice-hockey stick with a hook at the end,
For gouging grooves, or scraping horses'
Hooves:
Turner Prize winner, no doubt – entitled
'Runt Shovel, Aborted'.

We must assume it fit for purpose, I suppose,
But precisely what was that fish-knife's
Intricate task? The fish being already dead,
That toy harpoon was late to the feast, no
Better than a spoon for scooping lumps onto
Your fork.

Be honest with me: Are you one of those, who
Knows that the Emperor has no clothes, but
Dare not say – suspecting there is absolutely
Nothing expert, mystical or intricate in the
Task, eating a plate of fish – you are too
Damned civilised to ask?

'TOSCO'

Well before we can put words to it, are
We aware of ourselves, what we are, how
We compare with all the rest out there.
Their outside view of us, nothing new to us.
Within a quiet nonentity am I by nature
Circumscribed. Quite a pleasant chap
Really, but limited thus.
In my Thirties, it was once said of me,
"He's not going to set the world on fire".

The earliest candid assessment I can recall,
Came as a soft-looking 13-yr-old, in school:
The music teacher, from up North – 'Tosco',
We called him – pivoting his glasses upward
And parking them at his hairline, turned and
Fixed his gaze on me.
"Duz y'muther bairk?"
"Yes, sir."
"Av y'ever sin a lump o' dough?"
"Yes,sir."
"At's wot you lukelark."

SPINNING

Possibilities endless, from philosophical
To literal, in the dispelling of a darkness
By the light – kept before us evermore, by
Night-time following day and day-time
Following night.
For so much follows from spinning –
Spinning about axes, rotation, circling,
Orbiting; planets themselves, planets
Around suns, particles about their nuclei,
All as blindly as a moth will circle to a light.

At the spinning and circling of one full
Year, written on Christmas Day is this,
Metaphor most fundamental here, rebirth,
Reawakening, banishing of Darkness, by
The Light of Christ.

Yet they coincide at Christmastide, the
Pagan and the Christian, side by side,
At this turning of this earthly tide.

It is the Light of Reason, at this great
Hour of faithfulness, this festival of
Happiness, that dims awhile, in this
Light of Faith.

And though, as I suspect, Faith may
Be but Hope, apparelled in a fancy dress,
Witnessing such joy, in such a joyless
World, I'm bound to wonder, Light for
Light, if anything matters less.

RESTAURANT

Dear Restaurateur, hear me through;
I have some sound advice for you, to
Benefit us all: Among the reasons we
Come to dine with you, being on the
Verge of starvation is the least of all.
Fortunate are we, to live in a relatively
Prosperous land, famine-free, where
Groceries are plentiful. Daily, we are
Pretty well fed. A bit 'peckish' we may
Be – but frail and weak with hunger?
Not we.
We come to you, not to gobble down
Piles of grub, but to dine, to savour
Well-prepared food that we could rarely
Cook for ourselves. We come to you for
The 'occasion' of dining out with friends,
In the welcoming ambience of a well-
Appointed restaurant. How pleasant
It is, having fine food prepared for us,
And being served at table by courteous
Waiters. It is not hunger, that draws us.

Dear Restaurateur, let the 'starter' be
Simply that – 'amuse bouche', a brief
Taster, and not so filling as to leave no
Room for the 'main'. If you add bread,
Half a slice, not half a French roll: It is
Not hunger that draws us.
As to the 'main', do not overload our
Plate with veg or trimmings. Side plates
May help, but not with greens to feed
A family of five. Let a portion of chips
Be nine or ten, not forty; if we ask for
A couple of onion-rings, do not bring
A stack of eight. We are here for dining,
Not feeding.

You will surely find, Dear Restaurateur,
That the Chef will be delighted to see
Our emptied plates, and not excess food
To be thrown away.
 It will be more likely too, that my friends
And I will return from time to time, even
When we are not hungry, to dine with you.

TWO-SHOES

Out here, in the conscious world,
Morality is in the air we breathe –
How to conduct ourselves with regard
To others of our kind. The principle of
Treating others as one wishes to be
Treated, does seem sound, but beyond
The inter-personal, less we find, of
Common ground.
Along a broad continuum, is our path
Between saintliness and sin, so subjectively
 Spread that there is no point of inflection,
But a 'greyness' between the two, instead.
Here, within this middle ground, is this
Frailty to be found – a reluctance to stray
Too far from sin – for here are sweet temptations,
Forbidden Fruit. Appetites are but Nature's
Own, and where is the fun in saintliness?
Out here, in the conscious world, though
Morality's in the air, it's more convenient
Being bad, than good – the rationale becoming
Clear: We must avoid being too good.

While 'purify' is to cleanse, to refine,
'Puritan' would seem to mock itself,
Being a jibe of joylessness, pejorative
Every time.

Are you wondering, who prescribed
Morality's Rules – and did they take us
All for fools, yet why we should seem to
Shy away, from the very sight of righteousness?

For what use in the world, are those self-
Righteous prigs? What use, those Holy Joes,
Holier-than-Thou?

To be a carefree Bender-of-Rules, free-spirited
Libertine, or a spotless Goody-Two-Shoes:
Between these two, which might you choose?
In which direction are you drawn?

CONVERSATION

Scant conversation will there be, mainly
Talk, between High and Low, Rich and
Poor, Better and Worse; only as equals,
Shorn of such falsities, shall we converse.
Only when we meet on level terms, face
To face, may our conversation bear much
Fruit – such fruit to nourish the soul.

The space between us, face to face, will be
Want of understanding, having no dimension,
Not some territory to be gained or lost, but
A gap in understanding, to be crossed; not
A competition, but a meeting of minds.
It is but the human mind, with which we must
Engage, for all its limitations, likely to
Harbour so many thoughts fresh and new
To each of us.
On level terms only, face to face, may we
Engage.

Speak we neither 'at' the other, nor 'to'
The other, but with the other, please, in
Common cause of insight, truth, and
Understanding – that if voices ever are
Raised, it will pleasingly be in jest.

Dialogue only, must it be, turn by turn,
Whereof each may teach, and both may learn.

CARTOON

What has four limbs, two eyes, one
Mouth, two ears, and breathes air?
I know – we do, people, us, humans –
Oh, and every other mammal, large or
Small, upon this Earth – oh, and every
Single reptile too, apart I guess, from
A snake.
Good, a compelling comparison to make –
But don't forget those birds, in their untold
Millions – two eyes, one mouth, two ears,
Breathing air – and of their four limbs, the
Front two for flapping and the backward
Two for standing up. More than standing
Up, they move around on them, many by
Hopping but look, how many actually walk,
Just as you and I do.
Such fodder for the cartoonist, as if there
Were heredity here. Mammals, reptiles,
Birds, for every cartoonist tailor-made;
Added to his skill, anthropomorphism
His stock-in-trade.

Stand them up, in human clothes, with
Half-human faces, and have them speak
Our human words – fallible, as prone to
Mishaps as are we.

Not all about sketching, drawing, is this
Word 'cartoon', but reducing impressions
From the volumes of our minds, to two-
Dimensional images on paper.
Consider what sketches can do, all in the
Name of 'cartoon', all the way from sublime
Preparatory sketches, from such as Leonardo,
To modern political 'cartoons', with all their
Merciless caricature – all, in a narcissistic way,
Considering ourselves, reflections on ourselves.

Cartoons as people-watching: Along with Drama,
Classics, Mythology, Literature, Music, Painting,
Et cetera, Cartoons as People-watching, day-by-day.

NOMINATIONS

Another year now drawing to a close, we
Must honour and give thanks to those
Outstanding and selfless people – actors
And actresses good at acting, and players
Good at sport, who so enrich our lives.
As of today, and henceforth, public opinion
Insists that thanksgivings must be more
Widely spread; heroines and heroes long
Unsung, must, henceforth be sung.
Shortlist nominations are invited, therefore,
In the following categories:

Most law-abiding Police Officer
(golden handcuffs)
Detective Personality of the Year

Holiest Preacher
(embossed chasuble)
Best Supporting Preacher
Churchwarden Personality of the Year

Most Discerning Judge
(silver wig)
Best Supporting Lawyer

Dental Personality of the Year

Most Impartial Referee
(golden whistle)

Advertiser Personality if the Year

Most Erudite Professor
(iridescent gown)

Courteous Waiter Personality of the Year

Banking Personality of the Year
Best Supporting Banker

Most Dispassionate Butcher
Best Supporting Butcher

You are reminded that Lifetime Achievement
Awards are applicable in all categories, and
That further categories must be added by and
By, in the name of fairness.

Details of Award Ceremonies, to be spread
Over December and the New Year, will be
Communicated later.

ALIAS

To conjure up yonder-worlds for
Ourselves, we have such abiding need,
As to make one wonder at this form of
Hunger, which our daily lives inadequately
Feed. Leaving behind the fairytales, the
Wonderlands of infancy, we never do
Escape a quest for yonder-worlds, as
Humankind.
Go to the cinema, and sit there in the dark,
Gazing up to a world where elevated people
Lead elevated lives of those old Hollywood
Days, where 'Stars' in their firmament so
Wonderfully shine. Yes, that is the word –
Stars, in that celestial sky, where Earthbound
Names simply will not fly. No pseudonyms
These, as for authors in disguise, but names
To attach a pair of wings to actresses and
Actors in those Hollywood skies.
"I agree with the Director, you know; this
Will be the most romantic scene in the most
Romantic movie we've ever made."

"There's just one thing that bugs me though,
Those names."
"What of those names?"
"Well, he could hardy be a more impressive
And handsome leading man, nor she a more
Radiant leading lady – but Roy Scherer? and
Norma Mortenson? It's been suggested that
'Rock Hudson' and 'Marylin Monroe' would
Surely in this context, work the better.

Oh, and that big fellow, Morrison, is just the
Type we need in our Westerns – fighting off
The Apache, and punching the lights out of
The Baddies in saloon scenes, but I'm not so
Sure about the name."
"What of the name?"
"Well think how it will look on the billboards –
'Starring Marion Morrison' – they suggest a
Tougher, punchier name, like 'John Wayne'.

Oh, and while we're on names, Casting has
Been querying the name of that kid Frances,
With that wonderful voice, who's playing
Dorothy for us, and singing 'Over the Rainbow'
For us: Frances Gumm, they say – not quite as
Fitting for the world of Oz, as is her voice.
They're suggesting instead, 'Judy Garland'."

Or go to the ballet, and sit there in the dark;
Surrender to the music and the evocations of
The dance, weaving for us all its yonder-worlds.
As in the cinema, in this celestial sky, our
Earthbound names simply will not fly.
In Swan Lake, for example – a trance within
A trance – how can a prima ballerina lead us
There, through her dance, with a name like
Margaret Hookham? We can lift the Margaret
Into 'Margot', but for goodness sake, Hookham
Is impossibly plain: Odette-Odile has to be
Danced by 'Margot Fonteyn'.

No more could Margaret's successor, as prima
Ballerina, Marnie Crittle, keep her name.
Marnie who? Oh, you may have known her
As Darcy Bussell.

In view of our abiding need, to surf with
Those Stars, or float with those swans, our
Earthbound names we must adapt awhile,
Native to that dreamy other side – where
We may offer ourselves, where we may
Softly glide.

CROSSING

All drivers and pedestrians know full
Well, that a Zebra crossing on the road,
According to our Highway Code, gives
Precedence to those people crossing.
I refer not to 'pelican' or 'puffin' crossings,
Controlled by green and red lights, but
To crossings under your control, and mine.
Reasonable enough is this; motorists are
Recent upstarts; we were walking a few
Million years before we drove cars.

Too many of our policies and laws, it seems
To me, fall short by running counter to, not
Consistent with, human nature. Yet this
Provision does bring out our very best, and
So deserves our general blessing.
While both driver and pedestrian are at
Inconvenience here, pursuing their separate
Interests, with very rare exceptions the
Precedence works, graciously well – so many
Of us, drivers one day, pedestrians the next.

Along with common sense and practicality
In the Rule, every day we see mutual courtesy
And respect. Far from being set at odds by
Such a Rule, we are as one community more
Closely bound, for there is satisfaction in
Giving, hardly less than receiving, such courtesy.

Simply pause at the kerb, by the crossing;
That's all it will take. The traffic too, both ways,
Will pause, and you may proceed – and how
Much brighter will that moment be when you
Nod or give a wave of thanks, both ways.
Such simple civilities, such mutual respect,
Will lighten all our days.

EQUESTRIAN

"How is she, this morning?"

"In intensive care, heavily sedated –
Cracked ribs, pelvic fractures, neck in
A brace. You might expect such a fall
In the Grand National, but not in your
Local point-to-point race. She's getting
Round-the-clock supervision, by God's
Good grace. She's a tough one though;
I reckon she'll be OK.

"The sad thing is, that horses were her
Life. She lived and loved her horses, never
Happier than in the saddle. How is her
Favourite horse?"

"Had to be put down, of course."

FENG SHUI

Representing 'Wind' and 'Water', these
Two Chinese words would seem to know
Of us, and being elemental, accept a certain
Helplessness within us – or why would it
Matter, where our furniture was placed, or
Whichever way the pieces faced?

When you first arranged the furniture in
Your living-room, you preferred it here, of
Course, rather than there, and facing not
That way but this. Something there was,
Intangible but something true, and personal
To you. Any other arrangement would not
Feel right, less comforting and simply would
Not do.

It's not just you, but pretty well true, in the
Whole of human kind: We know that we
Could just as well sit there, but it would not
Feel right; it has to be here.

If you carry a comb with you, from day to
Day, it surely will be in that same pocket
As yesterday – trouser pocket hip or left or
Right; jacket inside, outside, left or right
Today, it surely will be as yesterday, though
From any other pocket it would adequately
Comb your hair.
Something similar may be said of where,
Invariably, you keep your handkerchief,
Your cards, your cash, your medication, your
Mobile phone and your keys – everything
To hand, so necessary to your day, are these.
Creatures of helpless habit are we.

As being elemental, those two Chinese words
Would seem to know of us – for there are
Elemental aspects of ourselves, into which
Each and every preference delves.

FODDER

Why one collective noun for rooks is a
'Parliament', is easy enough to understand;
Their habit is assembly, their vocalising
Unmistakeable, up and down the land —
Gregarious, of course as must any creature
Be, to warrant a collective noun. And so
Intrigued was I, to discover one for crows,
A 'murder', no less: How, a collective
Noun for a creature that does not 'collect',
Rarely seen but in ones or twos or threes?
Less rook am I, than crow, by nurture if
Not Nature, little inclined to vocalise, —
Even less to murder, I'll have you know.

Today, I have been watching from my window
A local parliament of rooks, gleaning in the
Field. With so many ewes in the field, two
Hundred or more, awaiting lambing time,
Supplementary feeds are scattered for them
Each day.

Though rooks predominate, several Jackdaws
Can be seen amongst them; some mutual
Advantage there must be, between these
Corvid cousins.
The ewes have flocked behind the tractor,
Hungry for the granular supplement dispensed
Around the field. Two things I remark, now
That they have taken most of what they can.

The first is the parliament, itself some two
Hundred strong, having witnessed all, drifting
Down for the gleaning, to supplement their own
Diet of invertebrates. The pointed bills of corvids
Probe what has fallen beyond the reach of sheep,
Even in a well-grazed field.
I see rooky-black lines and curves around the
Field, tracing the course that tractor steered.

The second, often observed, and watched
Repeatedly today, is one of those awesome
Reminders of deep provenance.

In spite of their compulsive drive for food –
Every few minutes those birds rise and scatter,
As if in panic. They circle and glide for a while,
Before returning to forage and glean again.
Some imprinted alarm, some inborn prompting,
Keeps them safe and wary – as of a guardian
Spirit from ages past. I feel sure it is through
Some kindred history, that I witness these events
With such an abiding interest.

A little later, descend the gulls, black-headed
Gulls, though still in their winter plumage.
With rather less flap than the rooks, they seem
To surf the breeze with a graceful ease. One,
Rather bland, collective noun for gulls, is a 'colony'.
For this least coastal of species, I'd prefer a 'drift' or
A 'snowing'. Forty or fifty just now, they arrive
Less for any grain, than for insects or worms.
They like to 'paddle' with their feet, that extra
Titbits may be raised.

Less nervous than the crows, they still keep
A watchful eye, with a distinctively smoother
Gait in covering the ground: At this distance,
I cannot make out their legs; they appear to
Drift around on wheels.

Springtime after springtime, these consequences
Pass; such tales are told. Ewes, we domesticate,
Simply that their sweet lambs we may use, on
Our dinner plates, our fodder – that we may feed
Ourselves and our progeny – no less a worthy
Quest than that of every rook and gull, to provide
For every chick in every nest.

There must be a collective noun, which embraces
Us all.

TEARS

Perhaps it was our withdrawal from
That old spontaneous mode of life, that
Gave rise to these, our tears. From this
Distance, I can only speculate.
Becoming too self-conscious to screech or
Whine or howl, to beat our chest or bare
Our fangs, we found ourselves distilling
Within us that which expresses, exposes
Itself, in modern times, as tears.

They need not be of agony or grief, our
Tears – we can 'cry' with joy – and see
How young children at a Birthday party
Will, from over-excitement, succumb to
Tears.
These emotions of ours are not always what
We care to make known, and have a way of
Embarrassing us, in tears, though they express,
Or because they express, truths. It is from
This civilised 'stillness' within us, that we
Can be 'moved' to tears.

So much more robust, I imagine, once,
Were we, screeching it all out.

So inwardly drawn now, are we, within
This, our humanity, that this fluid, for the
Refreshing of mammalian eyes, does, by
Some deep alchemy, dissolve, from the
Immaterial, substance in tears.

Tears may be merely tears, but as involuntary
'Sobbings' and 'dissolvings' of pent-up
Feelings of any kind, they surely help us
Along our way, saying what we otherwise
Could not say.

ERNIE

Something I've just recalled, from
A lifetime ago, I cannot resist passing
On now.

In a letter to a newspaper, I saw a
Piece by a primary-school teacher,
Who'd had a boy in her class
Evidently unacquainted with soap
And water.

She had written to his mother, as
Tactfully as she could, about the
Disagreeable odour, affecting other
Pupils.

The mother's reply was brief, and
To the point:
"Our Ernie ain't no rose.
Learn 'im, don't smell 'im."

ON AIR

In years of listening to familiar voices
On the radio, what I did not know was
That I was forming, unconsciously, in
My mind, almost visual expectations
Of what those people look like, face to
Face. The very tones of voice, emphases,
Enunciation, pace of speech, articulacy,
Would seem to suggest a type of face, a
Bearing, a demeanour, a personality no
Less, even something as unlikely as height
Or weight.
It is only when I see them, on television,
Or photographed in the press, that I see
How wide of the mark my imaginings were.
Moreover it is, oddly, a bit disappointing;
They are not quite as they should look.
I suppose it all draws from comparisons:
I've known people who sounded like that.
But then, most people talking on the radio
Are not speaking as they would daily speak
Off air, naturally, when face to face.

It is not personality, but persona, that we
Hear, so often in this broadcasting age.
It is not quite theatre, but kindred so. The
Sound media, in their many forms, so
Separate persona from the person. In our
Minds, I guess, we filter the one from the
Other.

The less the broadcaster preens himself, the
Less he addresses us instead of talking to us,
The truer our imaginings. More and more
These days, those behind the microphone are
As themselves, for which I give thanks.
We'll never envisage the physical person all
That well, but we'll see the personality more
Clearly.

SUPERLATIVE

This splendid word, 'Superlative' –
Supreme, unrivalled – first lodged in my
Mind in primary school. Miss Thomas
Was teaching us forms of adjectives.
She would give us an adjective, and
Invite us to supply comparative and
Superlative: 'Warm' – warmer, warmest;
'Late' – later, latest. Then, she laid a
Trap for the unwary, giving us the word
'Bad'. From the forest of urgent hands
Raised towards her, "Miss, Miss, Miss",
Pupils half out of their chairs, she selected
Sydney: "Bad, badder and baddest".

Comparative is the commoner, in usage
Day by day, superlatives weaving special
Spells, in the most remarkable way. Never
Mind who is better; who is the best of all –
Supreme, unrivalled?

To be good is always pleasing,
To be better, always commendable,
But nothing beats the best.
The appeal of competition, of winners,
Of champions, seems rooted within us.
That ancient notion of 'Bread and Circuses',
To keep the people occupied and entertained
Was so well-founded.

Nothing local, but a global phenomenon
In our kind is this, to find and celebrate
The fastest, the strongest, the most skilful
And successful – the best.
And see how fervently we attach ourselves
To our favourite team, sharing, in a way,
Its quest to be the best – joy when they win,
Depression when they lose. Week by week,
Something of ourselves, vicariously, we invest.
Did I say 'invest'? See how millions of pounds
Are changing hands in wages, transfer fees, and
Betting. In superlatives, there is money.

Add to this, eccentricity, weirdness, and folly –
A searching for fame, immortality even, in personal
Records – the longest fingernails, the most tattooed,
The heaviest carrot grown, the most 'Big Mac'
Burgers eaten in a lifetime, but of more sensible
Interest, the tallest man, the longest river, the
Largest earthworm, the longest-living tortoise.

Some Holy Grail of perfection, it would seem,
Haunts us from within, the unrivalled, the
Supreme, the best that we can be, at once a
Challenge and a compliment, to the likes of
You and me.

SHAKESPEARE

Such an implied compliment it is, to
William Shakespeare, that four centuries
After his death, we continue to read and
Watch his Plays.
How they develop, how they end, we
Full well know, but again and again we
Turn to them, for in so many of their
Acts and Scenes, we perceive ourselves.
Through his wisdom, his wizardry in
Words, his awareness of us all – we
Perceive ourselves.
Productions of Macbeth have I seen –
Maybe eight or nine times. The weakest,
And most frustrating, was at Stratford,
For without the Three Witches, but
Three young children instead – the
Dialogue modified to suit – the whole
Tension of the Play was deflated.
It was an affront to the reputation of
Shakespeare.

This is a more modern, and far less
Forgivable fashion than staging his Plays,
With all their Elizabethan idioms and
Allusions, in 21st century settings and
Dress – the justification, that his work
Is inherently timeless – being precisely
The reason modern settings are not
Needed.

I read recently of a new production
At Stratford, for which the 'Porter'
Scene is being re-written, to be more
Amusing for modern audiences –
A tiresome, vexing liberty – an affront
Which should be an indictable offence
Against some Eternal Copyright.

The Royal Shakespeare Company,
Being Royal, we might expect to be
Unswervingly Loyal, to the man in
Whose name and reputation they trade.

To stage a Play to the best dramatic
Effect, is a Producer's task, not to amend
It to promote and satisfy himself. How
Dare he? What conceit and arrogance
It must take, to superimpose yourself
On a Shakespeare Play, and sell it as
A fake. Leave this man's works and words
Alone; write works and wordings of
Your own.

In the particular case of Macbeth, by all
Means adjust it here and there, write in
Your own bits here and there –
But Do Not You Ever Dare,
Do Not You Ever, Ever Dare,
To promote it as 'Macbeth'.
Call it by some other name, however much
Or little you amend — as West Side Story
Is to Romeo and Juliet.

And Do Not You Ever Dare,
Do Not You Ever, Ever Dare,
To attribute your disfigured version
To William Shakespeare.

ARMCHAIR

What a dependent, vulnerable thing, is
This new baby. He needs enfolding in
Complete security, supports to his head
And his back. Awaken his senses as
Gently as we can. Soft reassurances are
Due, out here, beyond the womb.

He will never remember these earliest of
Days, but something, akin to memory,
Will accompany him through life, in
Unexpected, incidental ways.
Much, much later, in retirement, if not
In middle age, something akin to memory
Will find him in his favourite armchair –
Every evening in his armchair – at the
Same time yielding and firm, comforting
And secure.

Some sort of remembrance it must be, of
All-dependent helplessness, his head and
His back supported, enfolded in its arms.

Even beyond a lover's embrace, this will
Be his resting place, as if to admit no safer
Rest, than in that earliest, motherly nest.

And if ever he should not sense her there,
If one day she is not quite there, he may
Feel safer, in a rocking-chair.

CATRINES

Sadly, it is a Society that must exist, for
Cruelty to animals so disfigures human
Kind: Truly deserving of Royal patronage
Is the RSPCA, and so commendable its
Work.
In a paper entitled 'Advice on Deterring Cats',
It recognises the nuisance of cats fouling
The gardens of neighbours, but points out
That "Cats are protected by law and are free
To roam ...into other people's gardens ..."
It then delicately adds, "It is understood that
Some may wish to deter other people's cats ..."
You're damn right we would.
It then lists a series of counter-measures – in
Its mission of preventing cruelty – that hapless
Householders may take.
These include "Shoo a cat away, by either
Shouting or clapping your hands", and
"Squirt water near the cat, not 'at' the cat"
(Heaven forbid).

I appeal to cat-owners nationwide —
Just as dog-owners are obliged to bag
Up their pets' droppings, in the public
Interest, the problem of dealing with
Your cats' droppings must be yours to
Solve, not ours.

Meanwhile, once I have located the home
Of any cat that night-fouls at my place, I am
Determined to creep into that garden by
Night, evacuate my bowels, and hope to be
Protected by the law.

INSIGHT

And for eleven pieces of silver, that
Seductress, Delilah, betrayed her lover
Samson: His strength lay in his hair.
Then, even robbed of his eyes, he saw
What she could not – even when rendered
Blind, so much more than muscular
Strength, is the strength of a person's
Mind.
"I gave my chosen people eyes, that they
May see, yet they see not. I gave my
Chosen people heads of hair, yet there be
Misunderstanding of hair, in that world of
Vanity Fair," so lamented our Good Lord.

The apostle Paul, perceiving that a crest is
Not a crown, expressed it rather well.
'If a man hath long hair, it is a shame unto
Him.' (For all his whiskers and his shaggy
Mane, it's a spurious authority he displays,
With much thinning out and balding in
His later days.)

'If a woman hath long hair, it is a glory
To her.' (The female of the species remains
Twice blest, with a crowning in the hair,
And a knowing, seeing mind.)
"For all of which I must thank you, Dear
Lord – for not giving ladies beards, for
Not rendering lovely ladies bald."

"Why, why, addresseth thou me, as Lord?"

"Did'st not Thou make ye Heaven and Earth?"

"Indeed I did – but there be no 'He' which
So created: I am the 'She' – Ultimate Female
Power. Down in Vanity Fair, it's often a
Matter of hair. It seemeth just, in rendering
Menfolk bald. In man, I feed his pride, to
Feel the stronger; in woman, I feed her knowing
Better, and living the longer. His thinnings-
Out and baldings are of special kind, his
Manly seeings, like his hairline, so receding,
Likening to blind."

"For see how Samson, for all his strength
Of muscle, limited in mind, brought down
The house upon the philistines, but upon
Himself as well.

Your womankind, my progeny, the female
Of your species, with an insight and an
Understanding so exceeding eyesight, so
Surpassing physical power, and with that
Radiance in her hair, has a truer tale to tell."

MY BROTHER

Any assessment of one's brother, one
Must write with delicacy – or what might
The brother have to say about me?
Wherever far and wide you seek, I dare
Say my brother is unique.
A bystander is he, a ponderer, a reader of
Biographies and the novels of Dickens, a
Partaker of life vicariously.
He is a private man. Somehow he has
Found an enviable peace of mind – calm,
Unhurried, apparently impervious to a
Troubling world. In his understanding
And devoted wife, Alison, he has chosen
Conspicuously well, crucial to his peace
Of mind.

Where others might fume in indignation, at
Injustice, he will stay detached, filing away
Thoughts in his mind's library – without an
Ounce of pomposity or pride about him.

A treasure-house within, there must be,
Of unspoken thoughts, unexpressed
Opinions, wanting only the confidence,
And the inclination, of course, to share
What must be well worth hearing.
So much more there is, I'd say, than ever
Sees the light of day.
Such a passive fellow – even less a fluent
Conversationalist than I – he will listen
Quietly through discussions, and come out
With a brief, potted philosophy at the end.

A world full of Alecs would be a world at
Peace, a harmless, well-meaning world of
Tolerance, reflection and courtesy.

Benign, thoughtful, well-meaning brother,
Dear Alec, I could wish none other.

CELANDINE

How softly it slips from the tongue, this
Word, that wild-flower name, Celandine.
Those Lesser Celandines, I have in mind,
Quiet cousins to the buttercups.
A little sleepier than the snowdrops, they
Rouse, hereabouts, February, early March –
A sprinkling of Spring, along the edges of
Lea Bailey lane.
They are never a surprise, but always a
Delight, keeping that promise, the returning
Of light. And the root of that word, that name
'Celandine', recalls the swallows; inseparable
From our Spring, their arrival here.

And so turns this Earth, counting our seasons,
Counting down our days: Oh, surely not:
How self-centred, to view the Universe thus.
Vast galaxies wheel and wander, endlessly
Oblivious to us.
Only in our human space do we wander –
Time, Memento Mori, exclusively ours.

To write of flowers sleeping, waking,
Keeping promises, would soon be to
Have them aware of their own mortality:
Perish that thought.

Sufficient let it be, to savour the Celandine,
To savour the Spring again, as they sparkle
Along the edge of old Lea Bailey lane.

RED INK

It was fitting that, in a place of learning,
I was able to pass on a lesson of my own,
Lastingly learned.
In a morning Assembly, I addressed a
Third-year group, some of whom had
Known that young girl my lesson concerned.

To say the least, the presentation of her
English homework was poor – handwriting
Careless, more like hurried scribble. In my
Teacher's red ink, I requested more care
And pride in her work.

The next time I called books in for marking,
Her presentation, to say the least, was
Equally poor – lazy work, handwriting
Barely legible. On an improvement to her
Work, and to her attitude, in my teacher's
Red ink, I insisted. Again and again, to say
The least, the girl appeared to make no effort,
Deaf to those tetchy red-ink exhortations of mine.

And so to the end of term, and the summer
Holidays.

It was a couple of years later, when I learned
That the girl had died. She had died of some
Dreadful disease of the brain.
To say the least I, for one, was mortified,
Somewhat ashamed of myself, and mortified.
The girl had been seriously ill, unable to
Control her writing fingers – and I, with my
Teacher's red ink, had been impatient, and
Cross with her.

Had I consulted her Form Tutor, and indeed
If her Form Tutor had known, I might some
Sympathy and some tolerance of that hapless
Young lady shown.

And so, to that third-year group, in that
Morning Assembly, I was able to pass on
This important, this crucial lesson learned:

Please be wary of passing judgment on
People. Be not too hasty to despise, or
Criticise – for you may not know, you
Almost certainly will not know – all
There is to know.

PATRON SAINT

By the lights we select, to show us the way,
Are we ourselves illuminated.
Saints, being the holiest and most revered
Of souls, abiding with God in Heaven –
What are Patron Saints but Christianity's
Lights to guide us and protect us on our way?

In our United Kingdom, they have emerged
From misty histories and folklore, as personified
Emblems to light the way, I'd say, and give
Us strength of purpose.
There persists, in this ever more secular country,
A Christian legacy through our Patron Saints:
Andrew was an apostle of Jesus; Patrick was
A Christian missionary, David a Christian bishop,
George martyred by the Romans for his Christian
Beliefs. Every time we fly our Union Flag, we
Honour our Patron Saints: The cross of St George
And the saltire crosses of St Andrew and St Patrick
Fly at mastheads to represent our people, our values.

On our calendars every year, their Feast Days
Are marked, for celebrations by the patriotic
And the faithful. These special services, these
Parades, the flaunting of symbols like the
Leek and the shamrock, do seem to unify, like
So many uniforms and badges – an avowal of
Loyalty and purpose.

That we must gather to ourselves, these Patron
Saints, is what I ponder – some unspoken dread,
Perhaps, of what lies yonder. Consciously or not,
The supernatural is of our making, and would
Seem to light the path which, perforce, humanity
Must be taking.

A I

As we might expect, being but
Humanoid apes, our intelligence puts
On many masks, from the primitive
And self-serving, to the gracious and
Sympathetic.
Therein lies capacity to deceive and
Lead astray, alongside that which
Volunteers for Charities, freely, every
Day. Though equally valid, the instinctive
And the reasoned, the wild and the
Cultured, are potentially at odds: Bear
Witness, when there is a dire shortage
Of food.
But as humanoid apes, this inborn
Software, let us say, derives, through the
Ages, from refinements of our senses,
Our nerve system circuitry, let us say.
And so, if imperfectly understood, our
Intelligence, we may say, is natural.

And so, at the thought of intelligence
Artificial, I feel uneasy.
Faintly humanoid, I guess, through its
Design and manufacture, it will lack
Our instinctual ape. With the natural
Removed, how may it work for us, how
Can it 'feel' for us? I write in a spirit of
Regret, and some despair.
If it can 'think' for itself, upon what
Instincts, heredity or experience may it
Form its thoughts? Will it be anything
More than logical computation?

Intelligence, detached from a parenting
Brain – likely to be orphaned, acting on
Its own behalf – seems a barren prospect,
To me. Surely better, a cultured ape,
Than mindlessness set free.

Let us not set loose this orphan spawn,
Of such humanoid recklessness born.